D

Travel and Tourism

ISSUES

Volume 156

Series Editor
Lisa Firth

Independence

First published by Independence
The Studio, High Green
Great Shelford
Cambridge CB22 5EG
England

© Independence 2008

British Library Cataloguing in Publication Data
Travel and Tourism – (Issues Series)
I. Firth, Lisa II. Series
338.4'791

ISBN 978 1 86168 443 1

Printed in Great Britain
MWL Print Group Ltd

Cover
The illustration on the front cover is by
Angelo Madrid.

CONTENTS

Chapter One: Tourism Trends

Trends in the travel industry for 2008	1
Travel trends 2006	3
Health and wellness holidays	4
Holidays are the latest status symbol	5
Brits left cold by tourist hot spots	6
Rise in specialist holidays	7
Key UK tourism facts	8
New Britain	9
Britain's smart travellers	11
Space tourism – the future of travel	12
Space 'sports car' will take tourists into orbit	14
FAQ: gap years	15
Are these the new colonialists?	16
Ditch (un)worthy gap year causes, VSO advises	19

What is ecotourism?	24
Climate change and tourism	25
Aviation's impact on the climate	26
Nature's 'doom' is tourist boom	27
Forget the carbon footprint, we want our summer sun	28
Climate change could bring tourists to UK – report	28
Lord, make us green tourists – but not just yet	29
British tourists among worst in world	31
Souvenir alert	32
Slum tours: a day trip too far?	33
Murder, genocide and war: the new tourist attractions	35
Debauchery tourism sets holiday trends	36
Child sex tourism	37
Child sex tourism – FAQs	38

Chapter Two: Responsible Travel

Taking tourism to task	20
Thoughts on tourism	21
Tourism and possible problems	22
Insider guide: sustainable tourism	22

Key Facts	40
Glossary	41
Index	42
Additional Resources	43
Acknowledgements	44

Useful information for readers

Dear Reader,

Issues: Travel and Tourism

Statistics show that Brits are taking more trips than ever before, looking for their perfect holiday experience. However, tourism has a dark side, with problems such as carbon emissions, child sex tourism, exploitation of local people and destruction of beauty spots just some of the issues laying in wait for the ethical tourist. This book provides an overview of current trends, and looks at tourist responsibility.

The purpose of *Issues*

Travel and Tourism is the one hundred and fifty-sixth volume in the **Issues** series. The aim of this series is to offer up-to-date information about important issues in our world. Whether you are a regular reader or new to the series, we do hope you find this book a useful overview of the many and complex issues involved in the topic.

Titles in the **Issues** series are resource books designed to be of especial use to those undertaking project work or requiring an overview of facts, opinions and information on a particular subject, particularly as a prelude to undertaking their own research.

The information in this book is not from a single author, publication or organisation; the value of this unique series lies in the fact that it presents information from a wide variety of sources, including:
⇨ Government reports and statistics
⇨ Newspaper articles and features
⇨ Information from think-tanks and policy institutes
⇨ Magazine features and surveys
⇨ Website material
⇨ Literature from lobby groups and charitable organisations.*

Critical evaluation

Because the information reprinted here is from a number of different sources, readers should bear in mind the origin of the text and whether the source is likely to have a particular bias or agenda when presenting information (just as they would if undertaking their own research). It is hoped that, as you read about the many aspects of the issues explored in this book, you will critically evaluate the information presented. It is important that you decide whether you are being presented with facts or opinions. Does the writer give a biased or an unbiased report? If an opinion is being expressed, do you agree with the writer?

Travel and Tourism offers a useful starting point for those who need convenient access to information about the many issues involved. However, it is only a starting point. Following each article is a URL to the relevant organisation's website, which you may wish to visit for further information.

Kind regards,

Lisa Firth
Editor, **Issues** series

** Please note that Independence Publishers has no political affiliations or opinions on the topics covered in the **Issues** series, and any views quoted in this book are not necessarily those of the publisher or its staff.*

Trends in the travel industry for 2008

Information from ABTA, the travel association

Nearly 70 million visits abroad were taken by UK residents in 2007. The number of UK residents' visits to Europe have broadly stayed the same, with early bookings to Portugal and Turkey doing particularly well for 2008. Travel to the US has gone up this year about 3%, which will make 2007 the second best year ever for the States, but the quickest growth in travel is to other long-haul destinations, which grew on average at about 10%.

Hot issues

Responsible tourism and climate change

The travel industry understands that, like every other industry sector, it has to take responsibility for its share of emissions. The most obvious way to do this is through carbon offsetting schemes, of which there are many including ABTA's own carbon reduction initiative – Reduce My Footprint – which encourages companies and individuals to avoid (non-essential activities), reduce (energy consumption), substitute (or switch to renewable sources of

ABTA
The Travel Association

energy) and offset what remains. But emissions trading may well supersede the need for offsetting schemes in the next few years. It is now also broadly understood that tourism can be damaging to destination environments and local communities and there are now many guidelines available and good practice examples for planners and tourism chiefs to follow to ensure that tourism is a force for good.

Airport security and queues

Congestion clogs the workings of airports in the south-east of Britain. Stepped-up security has been partly to blame and early in 2008 some airports will be allowed to relax some hand baggage restrictions. Terminal 5 in Heathrow will open in March alleviating some of the pressure, but arguments will still roll on about airport and runway expansion.

Dollar boosts demand

The weak dollar made an impression on the UK travelling public in 2007 and visitor numbers to the States rose by 3% in the 12 months up to September. Other destinations pegged to the dollar such as Mexico, the Caribbean and countries in South East Asia, have also reaped the benefits in terms of British visitors.

Mergers

'The big four', became 'the big two' in 2007 and the implications of having the two biggest tour operators in Europe based in the UK will be felt throughout 2008. Both have committed to continue to provide popular package holidays and expand their independent travel options.

Internet

User Generated Content with web 2.0 has preoccupied much of the online travel industry in 2007 and this is set to continue into 2008. The web has continued to provide travellers with seemingly unlimited choice. Consumers now expect to find everything they need on the net. With greater numbers of comparison sites, portals, online video information, travel blogs and online customer reviews, it's been increasingly important for travel companies to stand out from the crowd.

ABTA Member sites – of which there are now over 7,000 – have to follow specific rules on clarity and transparency.

Cruising

Cruising is one of the fastest-growing and most successful sectors in the travel industry. Ocean cruising has experienced a larger than predicted growth in 2007 and the number of

UK cruisers in 2008 is expected to reach 1.55 million – a 14% rise on 2007. This growth will be driven by another bumper year of launches. Eight ships will be launched in 2008 with the majority sailing within the Caribbean. The largest will be Royal Caribbean's *Independence of the Seas*, which will be launched in May, while *Ventura* from P&O Cruises, with attractions including a Marco Pierre White restaurant, will be launched in April.

Nearly 70 million visits abroad were taken by UK residents in 2007

Innovations still abound within cruising and ship designers push at what was thought possible. The sector drives up standards of customer service and new customers are impressed and surprised with the range of destinations – from Alaska to the Antarctic, the Caribbean to the Yangtze – and excursions, which can include adventures on a Harley Davidson, watching penguins, or a hike in the mountains.

The media spotlight fell on Arctic and Antarctic cruises in 2007 and despite the rough seas and the potentially dangerous nature of taking an expedition cruise in these wildernesses, there has been a great increase in popularity for them.

Ferries
As a result of changes made within the ferry industry, there has been renewed growth and interest in taking ferries. Customers enjoy short check-in times, and the convenience and freedom of having their own car.

Short breaks
The short breaks market has matured considerably, but new airline routes into Eastern Europe and to the hard-to-spell cities of Szczecin, Brno, and Ljubljana will open up the region further. Morocco, especially Marrakech, is becoming a popular short break destination as the bustling souks and cultural differences make

for a great and adventurous city break.

Travelling domestically for a short break is also increasingly attractive. With no long waits at the airport, unrivalled entertainment and culture and rising standards of accommodation and food a short break in Britain is very enjoyable. The historical city of York has been voted as our favourite British city this year, but it is far from alone in its historical heritage. Watch out for excitement around Liverpool as it becomes the European Capital of Culture in 2008.

Designer and luxury holidays
PriceWaterhouseCoopers reports that the luxury travel market has grown between 8 and 9% a year over the past few years and estimates that it is worth £5 billion in the UK. The absolute top end of premium travel continues to boom, particularly with the hire of private jets. With airport security meaning that a normal traveller has to spend at least three hours per trip in an airport, the 10-minute check in time of a private jet has become increasingly attractive to the rich and famous.

People are continuing to spend money on top-end holidays and every week new luxury and boutique hotels – often now design-led and eco-friendly – are opening up. All luxury

clients, whether they have time and money on their hands or those who are increasingly cash rich, but time poor, want both value for money and excellent service. As a result personal concierge services have started to appear alongside the huge variety of holidays appealing to this sector.

One of the top reasons clients buy luxury holidays is for special occasions – whether that's a wedding, honeymoon, anniversary or landmark birthday.

Beaches for relaxation are the number one request for luxury seekers, whether that's 'barefoot' or 'glitz', but often clients are looking for something more exciting for secondary breaks. Big sporting events have become popular along with luxury skiing, diving, sailing, golf and spa breaks. But increasingly 'experiential' holidays that are aspirational, exclusive and unknown are being sought. Round the world travel, going to Antarctica or finding gorillas in Uganda are not only expensive, but are literally quite difficult to do and deliberately do not appeal to everyone.
19 December 2007

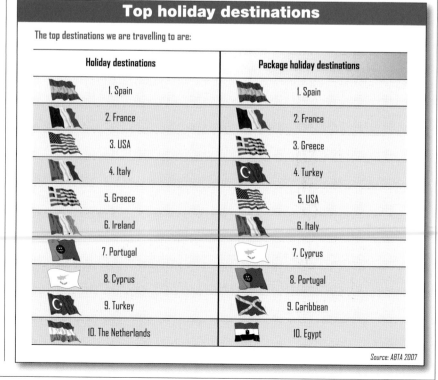

Top holiday destinations

The top destinations we are travelling to are:

Holiday destinations	Package holiday destinations
1. Spain	1. Spain
2. France	2. France
3. USA	3. Greece
4. Italy	4. Turkey
5. Greece	5. USA
6. Ireland	6. Italy
7. Portugal	7. Cyprus
8. Cyprus	8. Portugal
9. Turkey	9. Caribbean
10. The Netherlands	10. Egypt

Source: ABTA 2007

Travel trends 2006

Record number of tourist and short-term visits to & from the UK in 2006

There were a record number of tourist and business visits (that is, visits for less than 12 months) both to and from the United Kingdom in 2006, according to a report* published today by the Office for National Statistics.

Visits to the UK by overseas residents rose 9.2 per cent (to 32.7 million from 30.0 million in 2005) and UK residents' visits abroad rose 4.7 per cent (to 69.5 million from 66.4 million in 2005).

In 2006, the USA was the country with the most visits to the UK (3.9 million) followed by France, Germany, Irish Republic, Spain, Netherlands, Italy, Poland, Belgium and Australia. Poland was the country with the biggest increase in the number of visits to the UK between 2002 and 2006 (0.2 million to 1.3 million, an increase of 1.1 million) followed by Spain (an increase of 1.0 million), Germany (0.9 million) and France (0.6 million).

In 2006 over one-third of visits abroad were to Spain and France (14.4 million and 10.9 million respectively), but their proportion of the total number of visits is decreasing over time as other destinations become more popular. Visits to France fell by an average annual 2.7 per cent from 2002 to 2006 while visits to Greece, Mexico and Austria also declined over this period. In spite of a relatively low rate of growth in visits to Spain between 2002 and 2006, Spain had the largest absolute increase in visits (up by 1.9 million visits) followed by Poland (an increase of 1.1 million). Outside of Europe, India and Egypt had the strongest growth.

Travel Trends presents the main annual results of the International Passenger Survey (IPS) which collects information on travel to and from the UK. It is the key guide to tourist travel patterns and shows why and how people travelled, where they stayed and how much they spent. Note that this publication does not

national STATISTICS

address migration, either short-term or long-term. ONS produces separate publications relating to migration.

More key findings for 2006
Mode of travel
⇨ Air was by far the most used mode of travel, accounting for 75 per cent of visits to the UK and 81 per cent of visits abroad. Its dominance increased between 2005 and 2006 as trips made by air grew by 12 per cent to the UK and by 5.3 per cent for trips abroad.

In 2006, the USA was the country with the most visits to the UK

⇨ There was a rise of 3.9 per cent in sea travel between 2005 and 2006 (although neither sea nor channel tunnel travel is growing strongly in the long term).

Visits to the UK by overseas residents
⇨ Visits to the UK were fairly evenly split between three purposes: holiday, to visit friends or relatives, and business.
⇨ The average length of stay per visit to the UK in 2006 was eight nights.
⇨ Almost a half of visits to the UK (15.6 million) involved an overnight stay in London. Edinburgh (1.3 million overnight visits), Manchester (0.9 million) and Birmingham (0.8 million) were the next most-visited cities.
⇨ Seventy-one per cent of visits

to the UK were from European residents, 15 per cent from North America and 14 per cent from 'other countries'.
⇨ Those from Europe grew most, notably from Poland, Spain, and Germany. Outside of Europe, the USA and Australia had the largest growth from 2002.
⇨ There was variety between visits from the three regions of Europe, North America and 'other countries'. European and North American residents stayed seven nights and nine nights respectively on an average visit while those from 'other countries' stayed an average of 16 nights.

Almost a half of visits to the UK (15.6 million) involved an overnight stay in London

⇨ Those from North America and 'other countries' were much more likely than Europeans to visit London (nearly two-thirds of the former involved a stay in London, compared with 41 per cent of Europeans). Further, North Americans were more likely to visit Scotland.
⇨ North American residents spent most per day on visits to the UK: £82 compared with £53 by European residents and £56 by

residents of 'other countries'. An average visit from a North American resident involved nearly double the spend of an average visit from a European. However, the biggest spend per trip was from residents of 'other countries', due to their longer length of stay.

Visits abroad by UK residents

⇨ Compared with visits to the UK, visits abroad were much more likely to be for holiday (almost two-thirds of trips abroad were for this purpose) and almost a half (49 per cent) were for duration of 4-13 nights.

⇨ The average length of stay abroad in 2006 was ten nights.

⇨ Seventy-nine per cent of visits abroad by UK residents were to Europe, although that proportion is down slightly compared with 2002.

⇨ The countries visited for specific purposes showed quite strong variation. The Irish Republic, France, Spain and Poland were the top four countries visited for the purpose of visiting friends or relatives. For business trips the most-visited countries were France, Germany, USA and Irish Republic. For holidays Spain and France were the most popular, followed by Italy, USA, Greece, Irish Republic, Portugal, Turkey, Netherlands and Cyprus.

⇨ Forty-two per cent of holidays abroad by UK residents involved a package holiday. The percentage was highest (56 per cent) when holidaying in 'other countries', and lowest (35 per cent) when visiting North America.

⇨ Forty per cent of holidays in Europe were package but as travellers to Europe increasingly turn to independent holidays the number has declined from 17.8 million in 2002 to 14.9 million in 2006.

* Travel Trends is available free on the National Statistics website: www.statistics.gov.uk/statbase/Product.asp?vlnk=1391
23 January 2008

⇨ The above information is re-printed with kind permission from the Office for National Statistics. Visit www.statistics.gov.uk for more information.

Health and wellness holidays

Information from Mintel

Floating away on a holiday for a new you

Once British tourists were happy to return home from their hols with a suntan and a bottle of the local hooch. But today's holidaymakers are looking for so much more...a greater sense of well-being, a cleansed mind, body and soul or maybe even a new look. Indeed, latest research from Mintel finds that last year alone we went on no less than 205,000 health and wellness holidays,* where we benefited from the likes of yoga classes, holistic

healing, spa visits or even surgical recuperation. Indeed, in 2006 the British spent an estimated £135 million on these kinds of holidays and the fun doesn't stop there, with sales set to increase by as much as 150% by 2011.

'It seems many British tourists are developing a taste for a holiday with a difference. Tired of the fly and flop package deals, they are opting for spa holidays, holistic breaks or in some cases a medical break for a session of cosmetic surgery or dentistry. Although this is a niche market, health and wellness holidays are steadily growing into a high value business, with the average cost of a trip well in excess of the holiday market norms. This market is fuelled by those looking to escape the pressures of a culture of long working hours and what some operators see as an urge to retreat from the debilitating effects of the consumer society,' comments Richard Cope, senior travel analyst at Mintel.

Medical tourism: a cut above the rest?

Last year we spent around £25 million on overseas health and wellness holidays and twice this (£50 million) on UK domestic breaks of this nature. But, while once spending your holiday in a hospital bed was a bad thing, the largest sector of this market is overseas medical tourism. Although not strictly a leisure market, this sector is now worth as much as £60 million.

Medical tourism, which includes

cosmetic surgery, operations or simply post-op recuperation, has been growing in popularity over the last decade. And while most travel companies are wary of the risks of involvement in anything surgical, our research shows that more than one in ten (12%) British adults would consider having surgery or an operation abroad because it is cheaper, and as many as a quarter (25%) would be interested in recuperating in a hotel after an illness or operation.

'It seems many British tourists are developing a taste for a holiday with a difference'

'Demand for medical tourism was initially fuelled by a rising interest in cosmetic surgery, which is more cheaply available abroad. Today, this sector is a thriving industry as a growing number of well-off baby boomers take their health needs into their own hands and pursue the elixir of eternal youth,' explains Richard Cope.

Spa, spa away

Mintel's research shows that health and wellness holidays have really captured the nation's imagination. Up to a third (33%) of consumers have tried spa-type treatments, saunas or jacuzzis on their holidays within the last 12 months alone. Meanwhile, as many as one in four (24%) have had a massage while on holiday. This is significantly higher than those who have had these treatments as part of their normal daily life. What is more, no longer the sole domain of well-heeled women, men are now just as keen on these treatments as women. Metrosexuality is scarcely a talking point any longer. It is now the norm.

Mintel's Health and Wellness Holidays report includes real-life consumer video footage provided by Vox Pops, bringing to life Mintel insights and consumer analysis. By introducing video, Mintel reports will offer a truly three-dimensional picture of UK consumers.

About Mintel

Mintel is a leading global supplier of consumer, product and media intelligence. For more than 35 years, Mintel has provided insight into key worldwide trends, offering unique data that directly impacts client success. With offices in Chicago, London, Belfast and Sydney, Mintel has forged a unique reputation as a world-renowned business brand. For more information on Mintel, please visit www.mintel.com.

* Health and wellness holidays include fitness, mental and physical relaxation, medical treatments, beauty treatments, spa visits, mineral and thermal baths, health farms and surgical recuperation.
April 2007

⇨ The above information is re-printed with kind permission from Mintel. Visit www.mintel.com for more information.

© Mintel

Holidays are the latest status symbol

Many use them to impress friends and family

Nearly a quarter of holidaymakers splash out on upgrades so they can brag to their friends, but many tourists still fib about their overseas trips, it was revealed today.

As many as 22 per cent of holidaymakers spend an average of £300 each to secure flight, hotel and hire-car upgrades, a survey from Halifax Travel Insurance showed.

Tourists from Greater London spend the most (£553) on such upgrades, while those in the north-east of England and Yorkshire and Humberside fork out the least (£112).

The top holiday fib is the quality of weather abroad, with 9 per cent telling lies about glorious sunshine that did not, in fact, materialise.

Hollywood celebrities

Also, 6 per cent are less than honest about how they have kept in trim during their break away.

Around 12 per cent of Britons are envious of the places their friends visit, but 67 per cent are turned off by people bragging about how much they have spent on their trip.

Paul Birkhead, of Halifax Travel Insurance, said: 'Millions of Britons are purchasing holidays to impress their peers at work and at home. Holidays have become the new Rolex or Porsche, a status symbol used to impress friends, family and colleagues.

'Many Britons even feel the need to tell tales of meeting Hollywood celebrities and rock stars to impress their friends.'

These are the things holidaying Britons are most likely to fib about:
⇨ Quality of the weather
⇨ Bargain clothing buys
⇨ Restaurants visited
⇨ Class of hotel
⇨ Cost of holiday purchases
⇨ Weight-loss abroad
⇨ Resorts visited
⇨ Beauty of natural landmarks
⇨ Holiday romances
⇨ Celebrities encountered.

© The Press Association, All Rights Reserved.

Brits left cold by tourist hot spots

Research reveals Eiffel Tower and Stonehenge top blacklist of most disappointing sightseeing spots

The Eiffel Tower and Stonehenge are the tourist 'hotspots' that leave the most Brits cold, according to research by Virgin Travel Insurance that reveals the most disappointing sights at home and abroad.

More than five million people visit the Eiffel Tower every year, but almost a quarter of British tourists have dubbed the world-famous Paris landmark a flop.

Leonardo Da Vinci's *Mona Lisa* in the Louvre, New York's Times Square, and Las Ramblas in Barcelona all feature in the top ten foreign spots that fail to live up to our expectations, while the Angel of the North, Blackpool Tower, and the Princess Diana Memorial make the blacklist in the UK.

The findings have been explained by travel expert Felice Hardy, who suggested reasons why Brits gave certain landmarks the thumbs down, and warned that visiting some of the world's most popular sightseeing spots was often more likely to leave us feeling stressed out and ripped-off, than inspired, thanks to pickpockets, endless crowds and expensive ticket prices.

She claimed Brits might be turned off by worst offender the Eiffel Tower because it was 'frustratingly overcrowded and overpriced', and admitted that many would consider Stonehenge 'just a load of old rocks'. She branded the *Mona Lisa* 'disappointingly small' and marked down Blackpool Tower for being 'a forlorn monument to yesterday'.

'Many tourist sights are overcrowded and disappointing'

Instead, Hardy reckons we should be using our imagination and heading off the beaten track to find the 'wow factor', and suggested hidden gems abroad such as the Treasury at Petra in Jordan, the Tarako Gorge in Taiwan, and the Cappadocia Caves in Turkey. Closer to home, Alnwick Castle in Northumberland, Holkham Bay in Norfolk and the Isle of Skye in Scotland are among the best of Britain's tourist sights.

'It's easy to be swayed by brochures that opt for the mainstream and focus on clichéd tourist sights around the world, but many of them are overcrowded and disappointing,' says Hardy.

'Pick carefully and don't always go for the obvious – natural phenomena are usually more exciting than the man-made, and can be wonderfully free of tourists.'

Jason Wyer-Smith, spokesperson for Virgin Travel Insurance, who commissioned the report, adds:

'It seems thousands of Brits are returning from their hard-earned holidays feeling a bit let down when famous tourist spots don't live up to expectation. The key to holiday heaven could well be seeking out the hidden gems rather than joining the crowds in holiday hell.'

See the full blacklist of Virgin Travel Insurance's Most Disappointing Sightseeing Spots below:

Virgin Travel Insurance's ten most disappointing sights
Overseas
1   The Eiffel Tower
2   The Louvre (*Mona Lisa*)
3   Times Square
4   Las Ramblas, Spain
5   Statue of Liberty
6   Spanish Steps, Rome
7   The White House
8   The Pyramids, Egypt
9   The Brandenburg Gate
10 The Leaning Tower of Pisa
UK

1 Stonehenge
2 Angel of the North
3 Blackpool Tower
4 Land's End
5 Princess Diana Memorial Fountain
6 The London Eye
7 Brighton Pier
8 Buckingham Palace
9 White Cliffs of Dover
10 Big Ben

Virgin Travel Insurance's top ten must-see sights

Overseas
1 The Treasury – Petra, Jordan
2 The Grand Canal, Venice, Italy
3 The Masai Mara, Kenya
4 Sydney Harbour Bridge, Australia
5 Taroko Gorge, Taiwan
6 Kings Canyon, Northern Territory, Australia
7 Cappadocia caves, Turkey
8 Lake Titicaca, Peru and Bolivia
9 Cable Beach, Broome, Western Australia
10 Jungfraujoch, Switzerland

UK
1 Alnwick Castle, Northumberland
2 Carrick-a-Rede Rope Bridge, County Antrim
3 The Royal Crescent, Bath
4 Shakespeare's Globe Theatre, Southwark, London
5 The Backs, Cambridge
6 Holkham Bay, Norfolk
7 Lyme Regis and the Jurassic Coast
8 Tate St Ives
9 Isle of Skye, Scotland
10 The Eden Project
17 August 2007

⇨ The above information is reprinted with kind permission from Virgin Travel Insurance. Visit www.virginmoney.com for more information.

Rise in specialist holidays

Travelzest report shows boom in special interest holidays

By Bev Fearis

Online bookings for special interest holidays are booming, according to a report by Travelzest.

The report, in association with the Centre for Future Studies, reveals that from 2002 to 2006 holiday packages fell by 8.9% and this drop is set to continue.

Chris Mottershead, chief executive of Travelzest, said: 'We're moving away from a mass market culture to one of unlimited choice.

'Through the internet, reaching small and specialist markets is now economical, an example being that about a quarter of Amazon's book sales come from titles outside their top 100,000 sellers.

'It's a similar story in the travel industry, with the biggest growth sectors being in specialist breaks such as activity, health and spa, nature and wildlife trips and escorted tours such as opera, cycling trips, dance, cooking or wine-tasting.'

Dr Frank Shaw, foresight director for the Centre of Future Studies, said: 'People are spending more money than ever before on life-enriching experiences, such as luxury "small indulgences" and travel trends reflect this.

'We are seeing much more sophisticated and confident travellers who care about the world around them and want authentic travel experiences.

'Both men and women are putting a high emphasis on "me time" and are looking to blend hobbies with their holidaymaking. That might mean arranging a trip to Verona and booking tickets to an opera at the same time. Travel companies need to be much more focused on individualism.'

'People are spending more money than ever before on life-enriching experiences'

The top 10 'niche' travel markets tipped to grow over the next five years are:
⇨ Learn-a-skill-in-the-sun (e.g. cooking, surfing, painting, salsa dancing);
⇨ Inner self escapes (e.g. yoga, meditation, spa);
⇨ Hobbies abroad (e.g. art, gardens, cycling);
⇨ Festivals & Fiestas (dance, opera, food & wine);
⇨ Eco-lifestyle;
⇨ Wildlife & nature tours;
⇨ Sports tourism (following teams and playing sport);
⇨ The home-from-home hotel;
⇨ Soft and extreme adventure;
⇨ Nip/ Tuck tourism.
16 May 2007

⇨ The above information is reprinted with kind permission from TravelMole. Visit www.travelmole.com for more information.

Key UK tourism facts

Information from VisitBritain

Tourism is one of the largest industries in the UK, accounting for 3.5% of the UK economy and worth approximately £85 billion in 2005 comprising:

Spending by overseas residents (£ billion)
⇨ Visits to the UK: 14.2
⇨ Fares to UK carriers: 2.8

Spending by domestic tourists (£ billion)
⇨ Trips of 1+ nights: 22.7
⇨ Day trips: 44.3
⇨ Rent for second ownership: 0.9

Inbound tourism to the UK

⇨ The 32.7 million overseas visitors who came in 2006 spent £16.0 billion in the UK. 2006 was a record year for UK inbound tourism both in terms of volume and value (in nominal terms).
⇨ Total visits for 2006 are 32.7 million visits, a 9% increase compared with 2005, with an increase of 12% in spending to £16.0 billion.
⇨ In 2006 the UK ranked sixth in the international tourism earnings league behind the USA, Spain, France, Italy and China.
⇨ The top five overseas markets for the UK in 2006 were:

Country	Visits (000)
USA	3,896
France	3,693
Germany	3,411
Irish Republic	2,909
Spain	1,981
Country	Spend (£m)
USA	2,908
Germany	1,093
France	1,055
Irish Republic	907
Spain	835

UK domestic tourism

⇨ Expenditure in 2005 (on overnight and day visits) is estimated to be over £68 billion.
⇨ In 2006 UK residents took:
↳ 53.3 million holidays of one

night or more spending £10.9 billion;
↳ 19.2 million overnight business trips spending £4.6 billion;

The 32.7 million overseas visitors who came in 2006 spent £16.0 billion in the UK

↳ 49.6 million overnight trips to friends and relatives spending £4.8 billion.

Employment

⇨ Over 2 million jobs are sustained by tourism activity in the UK, either directly or indirectly.
⇨ There are an estimated 1.4 million jobs directly related to tourism activity in the UK, some 5% of all people in employment in the UK.
⇨ Approximately 130,400 of these jobs are in self-employment.

Accommodation

⇨ In 2003, the turnover of the hotel industry was £10.9 billion. This represented an increase of 4% compared to 2002.
⇨ In 2006, average room occupancy for all serviced accommodation throughout the UK was 61% (up 2 percentage points from 2005). Average bedspace occupancy was 47% (an increase of 3 percentage points on 2005).

⇨ The above information is reprinted with kind permission from VisitBritain. Visit www.tourismtrade.org.uk for more information.

© VisitBritain

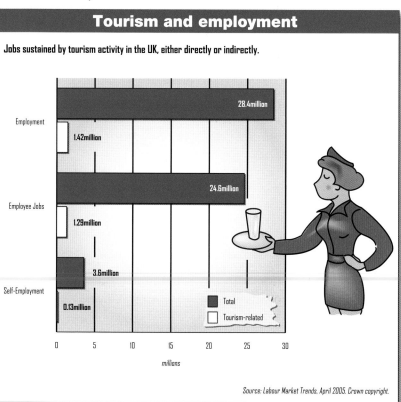

Tourism and employment

Jobs sustained by tourism activity in the UK, either directly or indirectly.

Employment
28.4million
1.42million

Employee Jobs
24.6million
1.29million

Self-Employment
3.6million
0.13million

Total
Tourism-related

0   5   10   15   20   25   30
millions

Source: Labour Market Trends, April 2005. Crown copyright.

New Britain

The changing face of Britain and its impact on tourism. Information from Lonely Planet

Britain is having an identity crisis. According to the new edition of Lonely Planet's *Great Britain* guide the growing independence of Scotland and Wales, along with the continued influx of people from around the world, has led the population to question whether they are British or whether they see themselves as English, Scottish or Welsh.

The 7th edition of *Great Britain* describes a cosmopolitan society which is heavily influenced by its multicultural population and where 'many are happy to revel in this diversity'. This has meant that 'It's difficult to generalise about a British national psyche – mainly because there isn't one!' (p60).

Coordinating author David Else said: 'although Britain's had a reputation for being multicultural for decades, this has escalated in recent years and the impact of these different cultures has become more widespread and significant'.

The guide explains how cities have been enhanced by Britain's diversity and multiculturalism. It states that Leicester has transformed itself into 'a vibrant, socially progressive melting pot. It has a large and vibrant Asian community with many interesting events staged around religious festivals such as Holi, Diwali and Eid-ul-Fitr' (p430). The guide also goes as far as saying that 'vibrant multiculturalism is a vital part of London's identity' (p112) and that Birmingham, 'Once a drab, grimy urban basket case... has spectacularly reinvented itself as a vibrant, cultural hot spot' (p408). However, David recognises, 'It is no longer just the big cities which are heavily influenced by other cultures, but every corner of the country. We are living in a global society, and the face of Britain has never looked more different.'

It's not just new cultures which are having an impact, the break-up of Britain's once solid union has also had an effect. The book says, 'if you look closely, it's Welsh and Scottish identities that are strong, whereas the distinction between "English" and "British" is a lot more fuzzy. In fact, many people in England have only started to consider an English (as opposed to British) national identity since Wales and Scotland achieved some political autonomy through the devolution process of the late 1990s' (p60).

Britain has become so cosmopolitan that visitors from around the world can come here and feel welcome and at ease

---

All these changes have had some positive effects. Britain has become so cosmopolitan that visitors from around the world can come here and feel welcome and at ease. As David explains, 'Brits are just as likely to tuck into a chicken madras as a Sunday roast, or to check out the Notting Hill Carnival rather than trooping the colour. Everyone can find something which suits them. Another great thing about our country is that being exposed to different religions, festivals, music and food, allows Brits to experience so many other cultures without even leaving the country. We need to revel in this diversity as this is the future of Britain.'

Other observations made in the book about the changing face of Britain include our ever-growing obsession with fame and celebrity. The book says, 'It is a telling indictment that more people vote in TV talent shows than for their country's leaders' (p36). In addition to being 'the fastest growing market in the world for internet porn' (p60), Brits also top the charts in the unhealthy eating stakes, consuming more junk-food and ready meals than the rest of Europe put together: 'without doubt, you can find great food in Britain. It's just that not all the Brits seem to like eating it' (p102).

What *Great Britain* says about...

BATH: One of Britain's most attractive cities...But it's not without its problems: the hills are knackering, the bars are snooty, the hotels are expensive, and the rush-hour traffic will have you weeping into your steering wheel, but despite all the niggles, it's impossible not to fall in love with this finely-wrought jewel in England's crown (p256).

Bath: one of Britain's most attractive cities

BIRMINGHAM: The familiar destructive brew of WWII bombs and woeful town planning left a legacy of concrete and ring roads that will probably never fully be disguised. But, no matter: Birmingham is making the most of what it's got. Established cultural and architectural gems dot the city centre and planners keep coming up with ever more innovative architectural makeovers: the striking postindustrial Bullring shopping centre is just the latest... More self-assured, cool and confident than it has been in many a year, it is hampered by only one thing – its inhabitants' accent, which is consistently voted England's least attractive (p408).

BOURNEMOUTH: It's a place with a rather strange split personality; part faded Victorian resort, part corporate anytown and part mass-market tourist holiday park, where wrinkly day-trippers and holidaying coach parties rub shoulders with stag parties, boozed-up clubbers and conference delegates (p275).

BRADFORD remains far removed from its much more glamorous neighbour, Leeds. Or so they would have you believe in Leeds. But even Bradford is getting a facial: much of the dour city centre is scheduled for a revamp which, according to town planners, will see it recast as an urban park with its very own lake in front of city hall (p513).

BRIGHTON: Family fun, high-brow culture, an exuberant gay population and cutting-edge club scene all mingle into one goodtime getaway not to miss. Don't listen to the folk that call Brighton little London-on-the-Sea. However cosmopolitan it has become, this is a place with a character and quirkiness all its own (p234).

BRISTOL: For years gritty, grimy old Bristol has been the ugly sister of Britain's cities, outclassed by Bath, outsmarted by London and upstaged by the rejuvenated cities of Newcastle and Manchester to the north. But the fortunes of this old industrial city have changed dramatically in recent years, and the transformation that's taken place over the last decade is pretty astonishing.

It's real, raw and just a little rough around the edges, but if you really want to know exactly where Britain's at right now, then Bristol is hard to beat (p245).

CAMBRIDGE: While you'll find all these qualities and more in 'the other place' (as rival Oxford is referred to here), Cambridge is the more concentrated of England's two great university cities, and in our humble opinion, far the prettier (p459).

CARDIFF: Contemporary Cardiff is the epitome of cool, pulsing with a creative energy and relaxed atmosphere that complements its youthful heritage ... historical gems, urban renovation, leafy parkland and

blistering nightlife are infused with a quiet nationalistic confidence and shoehorned into a city smaller than many of its English counterparts (p645).

EDINBURGH: It's the older and, with the seat of government here, bossier sister to Glasgow, and the two cities have enjoyed a sibling rivalry that has Glaswegians sneering that Edinburgh is 'No' real Scotland'. But she's a cosmopolitan miss, hosting royalty from the dreaded south as often as Scottish kings in her long history, with every other building wearing a royal tag. While Glasgow got its hands dirty with shipbuilding and the tobacco trade, Edinburgh went to university with the Scottish Enlightenment and became one of the most sophisticated cities in the world (p747).

Newcastle: a wild and crazy nightlife

GLASGOW: Scotland's biggest city is alive and kicking with a significant cultural contribution to make, particularly with a live music scene that's bound to have you on your feet and dancing (p781)... But Glasgow is no longer the rough little brother to Edinburgh's urbane older sister. The city is picking itself up and developing along the once-grim River Clyde faster than you can say 'urban renewal' (p784).

LEEDS struts across England's urban stage like John Travolta in *Saturday Night Fever*, oozing the confidence that befits the favourite child of the New Urban Revolution, that unassailable force that has turned punch-drunk post-industrial cities into visions of the future. And the future round these parts is all about retail (p508).

LONDON has a buzz unlike any other European city. It's fashion forward, ethnically diverse and artistically pioneering...London is sailing high on a wave of determination, optimism and glee (p112).

MANCHESTER: If ever London was to quit being capital – or was fired for some kind of terrible wrongdoing – Manchester would be a ready-made substitute with the necessary wherewithal to take on the job. It's a modern metropolis embracing change like few others in Europe; it's where much of the best music of the last couple of decades came from; and it has the world's best-supported football team (p556).

NEWCASTLE is still about the wild and crazy nightlife... take a moment to cherish the city's greatest strength: the locals. Geordies are a fiercely independent bunch (p619).

NEWQUAY: If Padstow is Cornwall's Cannes, then Newquay is its Costa del Sol (p331).

NOTTINGHAM today is a dynamic mix of medieval and modern. Amid multistorey car parks and who-cares-what-you-think architectural eyesores, you'll stumble upon a centuries-old landmark that crusaders probably knew – it's that kind of place (p435).

SHERWOOD FOREST: Don't expect to lose yourself like an outlaw: there are almost more tourists than trees in today's Sherwood Forest, although there are still peaceful spots to be found (p439).

SWANSEA: Modern Swansea is emerging as a serious rival to Cardiff, and the tiny, beach-rich Gower Peninsula is one of Wales' loveliest corners (p661)... 'ugly lovely' was how Dylan Thomas characterised his childhood hometown. Today, bar a handful of ill-conceived concrete eyesores, things have changed as the city heads full-speed into the 21st century. Admittedly Parisians, New Yorkers and Romans can sleep easy, but it's now perfectly possible to stay in the city and have a good time (p667).
22 May 2007

⇨ Reproduced with permission from the Lonely Planet website www.lonelyplanet.com
© 2008 *Lonely Planet Publications*

Britain's smart travellers

Information from TravelMole

Today's tourists are more likely to 'fly cheap and sleep expensive', travel further for shorter periods and seek out enriching experiences on their holidays, according to Expedia.

The online travel agency surveyed 14,000 customers from the UK and Europe as part of its Expedia TravelTrend Watch 2008 survey and discovered a very different breed of tourist emerging.

An increasing amount of travellers were happy to use the likes of Easyjet and Ryanair to reach their destination and then spend their money on four and five star accommodation

---

The survey said an increasing amount of travellers were happy to use the likes of Easyjet and Ryanair to reach their destination and then spend their money on four and five star accommodation when they got there. Some 46% of Brits chose to stay in four and five star hotels in the survey – double the amount of French travellers staying at the deluxe end.

Similarly, 'smart travellers' who are travelling long-haul will use their money to ensure their long plane journey is as comfortable as possible by upgrading or using the most comfortable airline they can find but will opt for budget accommodation once on the ground. Expedia considers half of its bookers to be smart travellers in 2008.

The research also highlighted the rise of the 'superbreak' which sees time-poor tourists travelling to mid-haul and long-haul destinations for short periods. Expedia puts this phenomenon down to the increased affordability of flights to far-flung destinations and 'the desire to make the most of even a few days holiday by experiencing something new and different'.

Almost a third (31%) of those polled have already or would think about taking a short break to a mid-haul destination. The most popular reason? To experience a different culture.

The survey adds: 'Our research indicates that gone are the days when you booked a package holiday and spent a week in the same resort. People now increasingly use their destination as a base from where they can explore the local area or even further afield by hiring a car or booking additional day trips. In 2007, searches for creative holiday activities via Expedia.co.uk increased – a trend which looks set to grow with a quarter of Expedia customers saying they plan to use their holiday in 2008 to learn a new skill or hobby.'

A new type of package holiday will also be popular in 2008, according to the report. Not the traditional package as we know it but instead a focus on booking airport transfers, car hire, city tours and theatre and attraction booking in a bid by travellers to maximise on available time at their destination. The site saw a 'significant rise' in holiday extras bookings in 2007. Some 21% of people now book a car at the same time as a hotel and flight, and almost a third (31%t) of travellers book previously organised excursions.
28 March 2008

⇨ The above information is reprinted with kind permission from TravelMole. Visit www.travelmole.com for more information.

© TravelMole

A quarter of Expedia customers say they plan to use their holiday in 2008 to learn a new skill or hobby

Space tourism – the future of travel

Richard Branson's race for space tourists – the Virgin boss reveals his plans to conquer the final frontier. Sophie Campbell reports

When Trevor Beattie was 11 years old, in Class 2a at Moseley School of Art in Birmingham, he did a project called 'The Space Race'.

He's still got it: a brown-paper covered masterpiece in blue fountain pen, sprinkled with illustrations, diagrams and yellowed cuttings taken from the Daily Mirror of April 1970, as the Apollo 13 astronauts circled the earth, fighting for their lives.

Tomorrow, Beattie, a 49-year-old advertising guru famous for his campaigns for French Connection and Wonderbra, will be in New York for the unveiling of the commercial sub-orbital spacecraft SpaceShipTwo.

Owned by Richard Branson's Virgin Galactic and nearing completion in California's Mojave Desert, it should take Beattie into space within the next 18 months, at a cost of £102,000.

It might not be EasyJet, but it is a start, says Beattie: 'It'll be a lot cheaper in 10 years. I think the unveiling will be a big moment. People will sit up and take notice.' Physicist Stephen Hawking is also planning a trip with Galactic after enjoying a gravity-free trip last year.

All over the world during the 1960s, little boys were glued to black-and-white television sets, as Yuri Gagarin became the first man in space and Buzz Aldrin and Neil Armstrong bounced on the Moon.

More than 40 years later, a highly successful and extremely wealthy group – Richard Branson, of Virgin; Jeff Bezos, of Amazon; Elon Musk, of PayPal; and the US hotelier Robert Bigelow – is driving the race to get us into space.

By 'us', I mean tourists, rather than professional astronauts. At the moment, there are only two ways to do it: for one – orbital – you have to be insanely rich; for the other – sub-orbital – just very rich.

The only paying astronauts to have gone into space so far – the California-based businessman Dennis Tito being the first and most famous – have done orbital trips with the US company Space Adventures.

> **[Virgin Galactic] might be dismissed as 'space tourism', but it could do for space travel what the Boeing 747 did for aviation**

These piggyback on the Russian Soyuz rockets that visit the International Space Station (ISS) twice yearly, and happen to have a spare seat, so that a 'private space explorer' can go up with two cosmonauts and spend almost a week at the ISS, doing basic experimental and maintenance work.

You float, you fly, you 'chase' the ISS, orbiting at more than 17,000mph, and you see 32 sunrises and sunsets every 24 hours. First, however, you have to spend six months training at Star City near Moscow, learn basic Russian and pay £15.3million.

Space travel with Virgin Galactic will be sub-orbital: the spacecraft will do a single, parabolic rocket flight into space and back, with views of Earth and four or five minutes of weightlessness – a trip of around two and a half hours.

It might be dismissed as 'space tourism', but it could do for space travel what the Boeing 747 did for aviation.

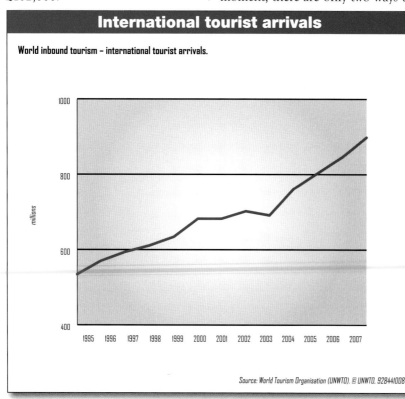

International tourist arrivals

World inbound tourism – international tourist arrivals.

millions

1000

800

600

400

1995 1996 1997 1998 1999 2000 2001 2002 2003 2004 2005 2006 2007

Source: World Tourism Organisation (UNWTO). © UNWTO, 928441008

'The flight of Dennis Tito was the watershed moment,' according to Eric Anderson, president of Space Adventures. 'Though it was a vast sum of money, it proved there was a market for space tourism. And investors started to put in money.'

Anousheh Ansari, an American-Iranian businesswoman whose family funded the $10million (£5million) X-Prize - to be awarded to 'the first team to build and fly privately a spacecraft capable of carrying three people to an altitude of 100km (62 miles) twice in a two-week period' - was the first female passenger with Space Adventures, just after her 40th birthday in September 2006.

Once she was weightless, she flew about too enthusiastically and was sick for almost 24 hours. The windows were small and there was no shower. She would go back tomorrow.

Writing a blog from the ISS - the first - she revelled in the smell of space ('like burned almond cookies'), the humbling sight of Earth, the difficulties of washing her long hair and watching the space shuttle Atlantis return home, 'first a flash of orange colour, then a steady point of light... toward the final stages it looked like a beautiful comet in slow motion'.

She is passionate about the future of space for human development, and believes tourism might be the key. 'The costs will drop as the flight numbers increase,' she argues, 'and demand for flights will be created by the tourism industry.'

Cue Richard Branson, who was a teenager when he watched the Apollo landings with his parents in 1969, and is hoping to take them - and his 22-year-old son Sam - on the first flight on SpaceShipTwo when it launches.

In 1999, Virgin executive Will Whitehorn had patented the Virgin Galactic name and was looking for ways to add space to the company's field of operations.

Meanwhile, in America, the Ansari family had started the X-Prize and the state of New Mexico - already linked to space through the Manhattan Project, and the supposed extraterrestrial visits to Roswell - had decided to build a spaceport on an 18,000-acre tract of ranch land next to White Sands Missile Range (apart from the White House, the only completely closed airspace in the country).

Two years later, Whitehorn was out in the Mojave, where Burt Rutan, the aerospace design expert, and his company Scaled Composites, were building a carbon composite plane.

'In the corner of the factory was a rocket,' Whitehorn remembers. 'I rang Richard and said, 'He's building a spaceship'.'

The spacecraft will do a single, parabolic rocket flight into space and back, with views of Earth and four or five minutes of weightlessness – a trip of around two and a half hours

---

It was SpaceShipOne, secretly funded by Paul Allen - the co-founder of Microsoft - which rocketed into history on October 4, 2004, winning the X-Prize. However, Allen wasn't interested in pursuing the project commercially, so Rutan needed a backer with vision and deep pockets.

By the time SpaceShipOne made its second, prize-winning flight, it was Virgin Galactic-branded, Branson had the commercial rights to the technology and Trevor Beattie had sent off his cheque.

Later this year, ground will be broken on the New Mexico spaceport, designed by Foster & Associates. Then, by 2009, the flights will start: after three days' training, the tourists will be strapped into SpaceShipTwo.

After take-off, slung beneath the carrier aircraft, WhiteKnightTwo, they will be able to walk around inside as they circle up to 50,000 feet. Then they will be dropped off into a short glide before the rocket fires, shooting them vertically to 68 miles (almost 110?km) above the Earth in 90 seconds.

The wings will flip into a 'shuttle-cock' position, steering the ship in an arc before it re-enters the atmosphere in a slow, low-friction glide. The experience promises huge windows and 'choreographed flying'.

Passengers will probably have flightsuits, though they aren't necessary, and possibly 'Nasa nappies' - there will be no loo and no food for such a short flight - and seats will lie flat on re-entry, to help bodies absorb the force of 6Gs (compared by astronauts to 'an elephant sitting on your chest') as painlessly as possible.

At around 70,000ft (21,336m), the craft will circle slowly down to land. WhiteKnightTwo has twin fuselages, each a replica of the spaceship cabin, so they can be used for training pilots and passengers, and for paying flights for people who don't want to go all the way to space. It will also be able to carry 30-ton loads.

In the first year, more people will go to space than have ever been (although that's only 460). By year three, there should be three aircraft and two spaceships in action. They intend to take these craft to different locations, including the Swedish Spaceport at Kiruna and, possibly, RAF Lossiemouth in Scotland.

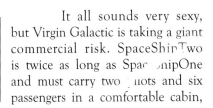

Could science fiction soon be science fact as space travel becomes a reality for adventurous tourists?

It all sounds very sexy, but Virgin Galactic is taking a giant commercial risk. SpaceShipTwo is twice as long as SpaceShipOne and must carry two pilots and six passengers in a comfortable cabin, rather than one pilot in a prototype. Testing will begin on the carrier plane in June and, if that is successful, there will be months of test flights ahead.

In the first year, more people will go to space than have ever been (although that's only 460). By year three, there should be three aircraft and two spaceships in action

---

Safety is paramount, morally and commercially; a space disaster involving paying passengers would be unthinkable. 'Burt Rutan won't hand this thing over until he would fly his children in it,' says Stephen Attenborough, commercial director of Galactic. 'And Richard is taking Sam on the first flight.'

But, as Nasa already knows to its cost, manned space travel is risky. Only last week, California safety inspectors fined Rutan's firm, Scaled Composites, and said in a report that the company had failed to train workers properly for a fuel system test that went wrong, when three died and three were seriously injured.

The explosion at a remote testing facility in the Mojave desert was part of the development of a new rocket motor for SpaceShipTwo.

Despite the risks, Virgin Galactic is not the only firm developing space tourism. While most billionaires with aerospace companies are working on payload vehicles, taking satellites or

Space 'sports car' will take tourists into orbit

By Bonnie Malkin and agencies

A Californian company has designed the ultimate getaway – a trip into space in a tiny rocket that can carry just two people; one pilot and one passenger.

The two-seat Lynx rocket ship is capable of suborbital flights to altitudes more than 37 miles above the earth.

The latest commercial venture in the growing space tourism sector, the craft is about the size of a small private plane, and could undertake several flights into orbit each day.

Its makers Xcor hope the Lynx will be ready to start flying in 2010.

But the cost of getting away from it all is not going to fit everyone's budget. Each flight is expected to cost about £50,000.

The Lynx, which has been likened to a space sports car, is designed to take off from a runway like a normal plane, reach a top speed of Mach 2 and an altitude of 200,000 feet (60,960 metres), then descend in a circling glide to a runway landing.

Its wings are located toward the rear of the fuselage, with vertical winglets at the tips.

Makers Xcor said the craft will be powered by clean-burning, fully reusable, liquid-fuel engines.

Xcor Chief Executive Officer Jeff Greason said in a statement: "We have designed this vehicle to operate much like a commercial aircraft".

Mr Greason said the Lynx will provide affordable access to space for individuals and researchers, and future versions will offer improved capabilities for research and commercial uses.

27 March 2008

other equipment into space, some have an eye on manned flight, and Robert Bigelow is even planning human habitats.

What President Kennedy would do if he knew that the space race involves a US company working with Russians and a British company planning to launch from American soil, we will never know.

But it's happening. Certainly, a lot of people – including the super-rich of Russia, China and India, who perhaps did their own school projects on space – will be watching the progress of SpaceShipTwo with interest.

22 January 2008

FAQ: gap years

Tom Griffiths, founder of gapyear.com, answers your most common questions about gap years

I want to take a gap year but my boyfriend isn't interested in travelling at all and wants to go to uni this year – how can I persuade him to come with me?
Would you rather persuade him to come and end up travelling with someone who doesn't really want to be there, or travel without him and each develop in your own way? If he doesn't want to go, don't force him. And don't listen to the cynics amongst your friends – loads of gappers manage to keep long-distance relationships going while they're travelling.

I'm taking a gap year and I want to travel for the whole time but I didn't have a part-time job while I was at college so I'm totally broke. How long will it take me to save up enough money to jet off?
You're looking at this the wrong way. Work out how much you have and how much you're capable of earning (remember you can work while you travel as well as before you go), and then decide on what you're going to do.

A cheap flight to Europe could cost you as little as £20, an InterRail ticket £150 or a round-the-world ticket £850. Then work out what you're going to spend when you're there. This can vary enormously, depending on how you choose to live. I once did a three-month trip across Canada and the US that cost me less than £500.

However, if you scrimp and save too much, you'll miss out on some treasures along the way. If this is your first trip, don't go for a whole year. Go for six months and do twice as much with your time!

How easy will it be to stay in contact with my family while I'm away?
The days of lonely backpackers and parents waiting anxiously for a letter are over. There are phones and internet cafes all over the globe, especially on the backpacker trail and in big towns. Get yourself an email account and make sure your family have one, too. Also, get them to sort out an international calling account – it will make calls abroad slightly less pocket-burning.

Why should I take a gap year – what will universities and employers think?
It's a fact that if you take a gap year, you're less likely to drop out of uni after your first year. Universities like students who take a gap year for this reason, and also because they tend to be more mature when they arrive at uni. Look around you during freshers' week – it's easy to tell those who've done a gap year from those who haven't!

A gap year could also help you bag your dream job. Employers no longer employ people solely on the basis of their qualifications. Life skills – such as decision making and living independently that you'll gain on your gap year – are seen as more important.

I've just got my exam results and decided to take a gap year before uni. Have I left it too late to organise a placement?
Absolutely not! There are lots of places left on organised placements: check out www.gapyear.com/clearing. And cheap flights don't kick in until after Christmas. So don't panic!

How do I know whether my gap year placement's going to be any good?
There are a number of questions you should ask your placement organisation before you sign up. You'll want to find out about travel arrangements, where you'll be staying and the work you'll be doing. Check out what training or preparation you'll receive and whether there'll be an English-speaking representative nearby. Get everything in writing, and ask to speak to someone who did the same placement last year.

What is a round-the-world ticket?
These are flexible flight tickets, set up for backpackers, which allow you to hop from country to country around the world. They last for up to 12 months, and are great value for money. If this is your first trip, I strongly advise you to look into RTW tickets. If you're dreaming of Oz, for example, an RTW ticket will let you take in loads of other countries on the way there and on the way back. For more info, visit www.gapyear.com/flights.

Do I need to go abroad to have a good time on my gap year? What cool stuff can I do in the UK?
The UK is full of opportunities that people never consider because they don't know what's out there. Chances are that there are stacks of cool things to do within 10 miles of your home, and you've only taken advantage of a fraction of them.

Volunteering is one option. Sounds dull? Ask yourself what do you love doing, and find a way to share it with others. Coach the kids' football team in your neighbourhood or design a website for a local homeless charity.

Check out do-it (www.do-it.org.uk) to search through thousands of local volunteering opportunities. CSV is another organisation that offers awesome opportunities, including media houses around the country where you can learn media skills. Year in Industry, the Prince's Trust and BTCV (a charity that works with people to bring about positive environmental change) can help you to have some top experiences.

⇨ The above information is reprinted with kind permission from TheSite. Visit www.thesite.org for more information.

© *TheSite*

Are these the new colonialists?

They're the students who go abroad to boost their CVs, have a laugh – and help out in the developing world at the same time. But this week a charity claimed that young people on gap-year trips risk doing more harm than good. We ask 10 volunteers what they think

By Patrick Barkham

Buoyed by three A-levels and a place at university, Jonty and Bunty and a quarter of a million of their mates set out to save the world. First they went climbing in Kathmandu. Then they stumbled into a local school and taught English to baffled Nepalese. Fifty spliffs and a thousand emails later, they returned home with a Hindu charm and tie-dye trousers. They had lots of great stories but the world remained thoroughly unsaved.

Gap years are having a rough time. Ageing cynics have long declared the term for the rite of passage between school and university refers to the empty space between the ears of overprivileged teenagers. Or the chasm between materialistic students dripping with iPods and the impoverished subjects of their misguided charity. This week, Voluntary Service Overseas (VSO) opined that the 'charity tourism' of many year-out programmes was a new form of colonialism. Students who travel to developing countries risk doing more harm than good, argued Judith Brodie, UK director of VSO, criticising the emphasis on volunteer enjoyment rather than on how to help the communities they work in.

Wealthy young westerners have traipsed off travelling ever since the grand tours of the Enlightenment. Now, instead of plundering the Elgin marbles, young idealists help run game parks in Africa (revealed this week to be the most popular volunteering gap year destination) or build bridges in Asia.

The year out has never quite shed its posh image. The charity Raleigh International – which sprang from a nautical youth project set up by Prince Charles and Colonel John Blashford-Snell – sent Prince William to help schoolchildren in Chile, where he struggled to explain to mystified pupils what a wombat was. Prince Harry also used his gap year to garner some positive PR by working in an orphanage in Lesotho. Almost half of all private-school pupils take gap years, compared with about one in five students overall, and eight out of 10 students who go travelling are actually from state schools.

Can teenagers tipsy on the excitement of both the Make Poverty History campaign and leaving home really help developing countries? 'Absolutely,' says Brodie. 'Young people bring a whole range of skills – flexibility, enthusiasm, commitment – and may already have experience of working with voluntary organisations. With well-planned programmes with clear objectives, young people can add great value in a number of ways.'

It is not feckless hedonism or misplaced idealism that VSO is criticising, but the booming industry in pre-packaged volunteering programmes. These are often run for a profit (although badly organised non-profit-making schemes may be just as harmful). 'This is a growth industry and very competitive so the objectives may not be to deliver the maximum benefits to the communities these young people are working in,' says Brodie.

Websites such as www.ethicalvolunteering.org can help volunteers to critically examine schemes. They should check what training they will receive, whether local people are involved in running the project, what proportion of their fees go to the communities they are helping and whether the project delivers lasting and sustainable benefits.

Andrew MacDowall, 23
Economic researcher

I had organised my teaching placement, or thought I had, at a school in India through a contact I met when I was trekking. We were picked up at the airport and the guy just said, 'So, you want to do some teaching?', and drove us to a local school. It was a ramshackle building with broken windows, and I don't know who looked more surprised – us or the head teacher who had no idea we were coming.

We were given books and some basic materials to help us teach English, but no training whatsoever. I was a terrible teacher. The syllabus was boring so I didn't stick to it – instead, I just answered all of their questions about life in Britain and helped them practise English. It was better than the existing English teaching in the school, which consisted of non-English speakers trying to read English books to them, so perhaps in the long term having me there was better than nothing. But showing them a map of Britain was probably a mistake, because they wanted to know what that big line through Ireland was. Trying to explain the Troubles to a group of 10-year-olds with limited English was tricky.

Historically, middle-class boys in khaki shorts have made their way in the Indian subcontinent. Now their grandsons are doing it with 'making a change' in mind, but where their colonialist forebears stayed in India, the modern generation return to their comfy homes in Leamington Spa. I really dislike the organised gap-year companies which clearly make a massive profit, and although I made mistakes with my volunteering, I learned a lot and I genuinely think I contributed to the school, despite my frankly inept teaching.

Sarah Cosser, 23
Trainee doctor

I went to Zimbabwe and spent a few weeks working in a hospital, but we were definitely tourists over there. I had been an auxiliary nurse in England and I didn't know if I wanted to be a doctor. It was a really useful experience for me, and the people were amazing but we didn't need to be there.

Later on, I did a two-month elective in India as part of my medical training, and I certainly wasn't going over there to rescue anyone. It made me realise that if I was going to practise medicine abroad, I would need to do it for a significant period because you need to be part of the community in order to do it properly. There are so many cultural subtleties that I would miss, and in India there are a lot of brilliantly educated people who understand the communities they are working with far better than doctors from the UK could. I worked in a mission hospital run by an elderly Indian doctor who refused to take foreign aid because he really felt the hospital should be run by and for the community.

I'm not sure how much difference an unskilled 18-year-old can make on a gap year. It's very different if you've got trained teachers, nurses or doctors. I met a Canadian obstetrician who was so up-to-date with modern practice he

was able to do a lot of really valuable teaching.

Tom Nicolson, 22
Currently working at
a school in Ecuador

I can see some evidence for the theory that gap-year people are the 'new colonialists'. Volunteers bring iPods and cameras to schools, so the gulf in wealth is quite visible. One of the first questions I got from a child here is, 'Tienes camera?', which means 'Do you have a camera?'

Students who travel to developing countries risk doing more harm than good

---

It was disheartening to have travelled 5,000 miles only to find that all I'm really here for now is money and assets. Everything we give to the children is snatched and more demanded. Should a child receive a new pencil, their friend will want the same privilege. There is aggression and so many kids will fight, lie and haggle to get what they want, be it fruit, chocolate or stationery.

There is also the question of whether we should be teaching them English in the first place. The native language here, Kitchwa, has already been squeezed out by Spanish. Because of our influence, children know what is out there to be had – the ugly behaviour of some of the children is comparable to spoilt children in the UK.

There is no doubt that being here has a positive influence to the bulk of the children, but the key is in finding the balance. In the past week, there has been a stop on sweets and sugar, and a ban on cameras and other western technology.

Some of the other volunteers, especially the 18- and 19-year-olds, are not really here for anything else than to go out and get drunk. There is a ridiculous mixture of people here. The charity needs the money, the kids are told they need help, but ultimately they are hindered by interference.

Careful consideration is necessary before we jump into these places with our size 12s. These children learn that their lives are crap where they are and it makes them want to move out.

Owen Callander, 23
Job seeker

I took six months out to go travelling and do some voluntary work. After trekking through Argentina and Patagonia I went to the Inti Wara Yassi animal refuge in Bolivia. I was working to rehabilitate monkeys brought in by the public to prepare them for life outside the centre. We had to pay to stay there, but it was clear the money was going to the refuge. There was an initial fee of $80 for the first two weeks, then $3 a day for lodgings thereafter.

I had heard about the refuge by word of mouth, and people were confident that it was a worthwhile place to work. It's an ongoing project, and there are always volunteers there. We had an amazing time, but we were up at 7.30am every day and working until 6pm. The focus was the work. I got a lot out of it, and I did feel I made a difference while I was there, but it wasn't about 'me', it was about the park and the fulfilment you get from working closely with the animals.

Anna Seligman, 21
Law student

I went to Tanzania with an organisation called Changing Worlds and worked in a boarding school for children aged 6-13. Originally, I just wanted to go travelling and see the world, but then I decided that I wanted to immerse myself in a different culture and see how other people lived. I also wanted to give something back. I am certain that I had a good short-term effect on the children – for one, when they were in my lessons, I didn't use the cane like their other teachers – and I hope that I had a long-lasting impact too.

I don't think people on gap years are the new colonialists; it depends on the individual. There was certainly one Brit in my group who kept going on about how good the experience would look on his CV, but at the end it became something much deeper for him, too.

Tommy Seddon, 21
English literature student

I was a little surprised to read that my gap year had helped create a new army of 'colonialists'. I spent the first six months of 2004 teaching English as a foreign language in Thali, a small village just outside of Kathmandu in Nepal. I had had a one-week course to 'train' me as a teacher, although upon arrival this turned out to be useless, as the resources we thought we might have (moveable desks, enough paper, classes small enough to organise group activities) were clearly not there. However, I learned to get by and taught as a language assistant, providing opportunities for children between the ages of 6 and 13 to try out their English, in addition to helping the teachers brush up on theirs. The school we worked at had received western volunteer teachers for a few years, including some who were second- or third-year students. My time abroad may have had an impact on the lives of the students, but I am almost certain it was a universally positive one.

Luke Waterson, 25
Press officer

I had an incredible, culturally enriching time, bouncing on buses through villages where westerners had seldom ever been seen. In Bolivia, I helped out in a local school assisting in overcrowded classrooms where there would be no assistance otherwise. Regardless of motivation, I gave back as much as I took to the countries I visited during my year in South America.

Tourism, good and bad, supports economies of developing nations. Plenty of our compatriots disgrace themselves and offend local people in the resorts of these nations, but other tourists genuinely wish to give something back and gap-year companies exist for this reason. Before, young people who wanted to broaden horizons by contributing positively towards other cultures did not know how to set about it. Now they do. A proportion of the money each volunteer pays these companies does go to fund essential projects in the host country. The unskilled students volunteering have willingness as a qualification. The financial contribution and the exchange of ideas and of languages establishes friendships and enlightens the lives of the people one encounters. Throwing pleasure into the package is an added incentive for young people who want to help others and enjoy themselves. It is difficult to be cynical about that.

Tom Howe, 23
Language school
activities coordinator

I worked for five months in Cuenca in Ecuador both teaching English and helping out at a project for street kids. During the week I taught in various schools in the mornings and in the afternoon I would go to a market where a Christian-run project had its premises. The kids who came there for their lunch were not literally street kids – they all had families – but they were very poor. We would serve them lunch and then help them with their homework afterwards, or sometimes play chess.

Apart from improving my Spanish, I felt I benefited a lot from having genuine contact with local people which you don't necessarily get when you are just travelling around. Interacting with locals and getting to know them stops you feeling like you are a visitor at a social zoo. I remember chatting to one old woman who was a cook at the project and she asked where I was from. When I said Britain she genuinely didn't know where that was. Part of the money I paid to the gap-year company subsidised the cost of an Ecuadorian coming to Britain for a year. I think this is a really good idea and helps counter the notion that gap years are neo-colonialist.

Dave Firth, 23
Newspaper sub-editor

I went travelling in Thailand, Australia and Hong Kong to see the world and have a good time. I'd just finished my A-levels and saved up £2,000, and I know it sounds selfish, but I wanted to spend it on myself. I went with four close friends, and for the first three weeks we all got on fine. After that, things descended into silly games that mainly involved jumping on every opportunity to hit each other. It was an amazing trip though, and I'm glad I put all of my energy into having fun. I think it will be almost impossible to do it again given my work commitments.

I know people who have gone off to developing countries to do voluntary work, and I have got a lot of respect for that. Going abroad to make a difference just wasn't what I wanted to do. I was 18 and needed to see something other than England. I may not have helped clean streets but I came back a much better person, genuinely feeling like I knew more about life. Maybe one day I will do some 'helpful' travelling, but whether or not you go with the intention to have an impact on a particular country, I think everyone needs to see a new part of the world for a few months at some point in their life.

Tom Sykes, 22
Pursuing a career
as a magician

I taught English to children in a small village in Tanzania for three and a half months. There were four of us volunteering and we worked quite hard. I paid a gap-year company £2,600 for the trip, so I certainly wasn't a drain on local resources. The money covered my flights and accommodation and a portion went to the school where I was. There were 100 kids in a class, so the school needed more teachers, but I know I got more out of the experience than if I had been teaching somewhere else. The children enjoyed my lessons and I would read them stories. I believe you can make a difference to people's lives.

We lived in a house with no water or electricity, but were still able to buy luxuries. Having money did separate us from the other teachers in some ways but we did socialise with them. They were very generous to include us in their plans and were too proud to ask us for anything materially. We cooked together and learned about each other's cultures.

⇨ Interviews by Helen Dowd, Helen Pidd and Lucy Clouting.

18 August 2006

Ditch (un)worthy gap year causes, VSO advises

Charity says a year spent travelling can be more beneficial than doing spurious voluntary work

Ahead of the publication of A-level results later this week, international development charity VSO is cautioning young people who are taking a gap year abroad that it may be better to travel rather than take up spurious voluntary work in developing countries.

The charity is concerned that young people are coming under increasing pressure to volunteer overseas during their gap year. While it encourages volunteering for people of all ages, it says that badly planned and supported 'voluntourism' schemes may be having a negative impact on young people and the communities they work with. It is advising young people who are serious about gap year voluntary work to carefully research who they go with and choose a development focused organisation.

Judith Brodie, Director of VSO UK, said:

'Spending your gap year volunteering overseas has become a rite of passage for young people and the gap year market has grown considerably. While there are many good gap year providers we are increasingly concerned about the number of badly planned and supported schemes that are spurious – ultimately benefiting no one apart from the travel companies that organise them. Young people want to make a difference through volunteering, but they would be better off travelling and experiencing different cultures, rather than wasting time on projects that have no impact and can leave a big hole in their wallet.'

Last year VSO warned that gappers risked becoming the new colonialists if attitudes to voluntary work in the developing world didn't change. It argued that the gap year market was increasingly catering to the needs of volunteers, rather than the communities they claim to support. It called for a radical rethink of gap years and urged providers to work with local communities to ensure young people are doing work that has a meaningful impact.

Hannah Saunders, 19, from London, took up a placement teaching in India with a commercial organisation:

'I paid over £1000 to teach English and maths to children in Pune. I didn't have any training or preparation from the organisation before I went, and they didn't expect me to have any qualifications. I had a really tough time and suffered from culture shock, as India is so different from anywhere else, which I wasn't ready for. I turned up at the learning centre and the teachers didn't even know I was coming. It was very hard to find out what I was supposed to be doing. It wasn't value for money, as there was very little support from the organisation before or during my time there.'

VSO is currently working with established gap year providers to devise a code of good practice to help would-be gappers weigh up their options. The charity has also devised a checklist designed to assess the providers' commitment to volunteering, the communities they work in, and the young people they work with.

Gap year checklist

If you're planning on heading overseas to volunteer ask the organisation you contact these questions before you decide:

1 Will you be given a defined role and purpose?
2 Will you meet face to face with your provider and attend a selection day to assess your suitability for the volunteering opportunities and gain detailed information about the structure of your placement?
3 How much will it cost and what does this pay for?
4 How will you be supported with training and personal development needs before, during and after your placement?
5 Is the work you do linked to long-term community partnerships that have a lasting impact? And how do volunteers work in partnership with the local community?
6 Does the organisation you are going with have established offices overseas that work in partnership with local people?
7 Can your organisation guarantee you 24-hour-a-day health, safety and security assistance?
8 Does the organisation have a commitment to diversity amongst its volunteers?
9 How does the organisation encourage long-term awareness of real development issues?
10 How will your work be monitored and evaluated so that others can build on what you have done?

Fact box

⇨ Up to 200,000 Britons take a gap year every year, 130,000 of them are school-leavers. (Year Out Group)
⇨ The British gap year travel market comprises approximately 1% of all UK outbound trips and around 10% of outbound travel expenditure. (Mintel)
⇨ The average gap year traveller spends around £4,800. (Mintel)

14 August 2007

⇨ The above information is reprinted with kind permission from Voluntary Service Overseas. Visit www.vso.org.uk for more information.

© VSO

Taking tourism to task

Information from the Economic and Social Research Council

By Judith Oliver

Is international tourism a tool for reducing global poverty or a source of greater inequality between rich and poor? That was the question discussed this week (22-23 June) by academics from across the globe, during a two-day tourism symposium hosted by the Centre for Tourism Policy Studies at the University of Brighton.

However, Professor David Hulme, Deputy Director of the ESRC Global Poverty Research Group (GPRG), feels he may already have the answer. He says: 'Tourism can make a significant contribution to growth, but because the benefits are distributed very unequally it makes a relatively small impact on poverty.' He gives the example of an African safari. 'Currently only one cent in the dollar of the cost of that safari feeds through to the people who actually live and work on the game reserve.'

In terms of the environment, the tourism scorecard is also pretty mixed. According to Professor Kerry Turner, Director of the ESRC's Centre for Social and Economic Research on the Global Environment (CSERGE), unconstrained tourism development in or near sensitive environments can result in severe air and water pollution and waste disposal problems, and it may lead to the eventual loss of tourism itself. He points out: 'The end state is an environment that is not fit for residents' or tourists' needs.'

On a more positive note, however, he argues that ecotourism (tourism managed on sustainability lines) can provide sustainable livelihoods and conserve valuable habitats, such as tropical forests and wetlands, for a variety of species.

Ecotourism can certainly provide better employment options than logging and mining, which are currently damaging the environment

in places such as Costa Rica, argues Dr Donald Macleod of Glasgow University's Crichton Tourism Research Centre (CTRC). His research into tourism in both the Canary Islands and Bali further identifies a range of cultural and social benefits, ranging from inhabitants' increased confidence in their local culture to greater opportunities to find work locally.

Indeed, the future could hold a fairer deal all round in terms of tourism. What would help, says Professor Hulme, is if tourism-related businesses adopted a greater sense of corporate social responsibility and helped local people to contribute more to tourist activities.

Even the environmental damage caused when tourists travel to their destinations could lessen in future, says Dr Daniel Osborn of the UK Energy Research Centre (UKERC). 'We can expect to see more biofuels becoming available in the next few years and these should help limit increases in the levels of carbon dioxide in the atmosphere. Such technological developments will help keep travel options open.'

However, issues still remain concerning the environmental impact of aeroplane vapour trails and the increase in the number of people flying. Nevertheless, UK residents can still enjoy the option of guilt-free tourism by taking their holidays closer to home. Dr Jeremy Phillipson, Assistant Director of the Rural Economy and Land Use Programme (RELU), which is co-funded by the ESRC, points to the vital role tourism plays in the UK's rural economy.

'Tourism is often a key driver of rural development. We saw this most

starkly in 2001 when foot-and-mouth disease led to a £3 billion loss to the sector,' he explains. 'Estimates suggest that in 2000 rural tourism attracted £14 billion and that its 25,000 or so businesses hosted 80 million visits and overnight stays from domestic visitors. Tourism has many linkages into other parts of the rural economy and, in many respects tourism and leisure can be seen to be key elements of the new rural economy.'

So, perhaps some Scottish midges instead of foreign bugs this year?
23 June 2006

⇨ The above information is reprinted with kind permission from the Economic and Social Research Council. Visit www.esrc.ac.uk for more information.

Thoughts on tourism

Mass tourism is both a force for good and a potential for harm

There is no doubt that the economies of many impoverished areas of the world have come to benefit hugely from tourism – after all, it is one of the three biggest industries on the planet!

In South-East Asia and the Indian subcontinent, this is increasingly noticeable. Just over a decade ago, many parts of Thailand, Malaysia, India, Vietnam, Cambodia, Laos, Indonesia and Sri Lanka were the domain of the backpackers, a secret known only to the afficionados of the Lonely Planet guide books. Today, those same areas have undergone rapid development, with investment in the tourist infrastructure benefiting many people.

Tourism dependency

However, in some areas, whole communities have now become dependent upon tourism because farming and traditional industries have been abandoned in favour of more lucrative tourism-linked activity. This means that when tourism declines, the economic sustainability of the whole community will also be undermined. This is why the impact of the December 04 Tsunami was so devastating. When the tourists didn't come - tourism workers were left without an income.

Furthermore, tourism has also had an impact upon the social fabric and the culture of many communities. In some areas the clash between traditional cultures and those of western tourists is noticeable, often with the western culture proving more dominant, and indigenous cultures threatened with dilution, or even extinction. After all, we have the money!

Our responsibility to be responsible

It is only right that when we relatively wealthy tourists enjoy the benefits of tourism, we should do so responsibly, by ensuring that we are not contributing to the exploitation of either people or the environment, that we are participating in 'fair trade' practices which benefit those who work so hard to make our holidays so great, that we are contributing to the sustainable economic development of the communities who host us, and that we are respectful towards and assist in the maintenance of indigenous cultures.

> There is no doubt that the economies of many impoverished areas of the world have come to benefit hugely from tourism

But how can you do this? Well, make sure tour operators have a responsible travel or ethical tourism policy - and that this policy is adhered to. Choose to go on holiday with a company who make sustainable tourism and fair trade travel as much of a priority as the quality of the accommodation or the cleanliness of the swimming pool. Finally join an organisation such as Tourism Concern, who campaign to make responsible tourism practices the mainstream norm for all, and not the exception for the few, and fight against exploitation by or for tourists!

Air travel – blessing or curse?

Finally, air travel contributes to high-level carbon dioxide emissions, a prime cause of global warming, which will have a drastic impact upon the environment within just a few decades if left unchecked. This not only includes global warming, but the rising acidity of the world's oceans - which is killing many species slowly, and decimating coral reefs all over the world.

Yet if governments decided to tax airline fuels to disincentivise air travel, it would be the developing countries dependent upon tourism which would be hit, and long-haul travel would again become the preserve of just the very wealthy - reducing the number of tourists able to visit the developing world.

Therefore, we suggest that we do something as individuals to counteract our environmental impact, by using some of our air fuel tax subsidy the governments currently don't charge us, to purchase and plant a tree, which will pay back our carbon debt to future generations.

⇨ The above information is reprinted with kind permission from Different Travel. Visit their website at www.different-travel.com for more information on this and other travel-related topics.

© Different Travel

Tourism and possible problems

Information from Global Gateway

While tourism can be a powerful positive force for change in poor countries, it can also be seriously damaging for the local environment and culture.

An increase in mass tourism that is not controlled responsibly can ruin areas of natural beauty. Tourism can damage coral reefs, pollute beaches and destroy the habitats of wildlife as roads and hotels are built. Ironically, damage to these natural resources is likely to reduce future numbers of visitors. Another negative effect is that the increasing numbers of aeroplane flights are a major cause of global warming.

A second problem is that the tourist resorts are frequently owned by large Western companies and all too often the profits earned from tourism go straight into the bank accounts of these companies. Moreover, the well-paid managerial positions are often held by foreigners, and the wages given to local hotel employees are usually very low. Where this is the case very little money enters the local economy at all. By purchasing souvenirs, food and other goods from local people you can help to spread the benefits of tourism.

Finally, tourism can have an adverse effect on local culture, traditions and the way of life. Large numbers of tourists can undermine traditional beliefs, values and customs and in particular risk commercialising the very culture that they find so interesting. And where these tourists are insensitive to local traditions their behaviour can cause great offence.

⇨ The above information is reprinted with kind permission from Global Gateway. Visit www.globalgateway. org for more information.

© Global Gateway

Insider guide: sustainable tourism

Travel that makes a positive difference

What is sustainable tourism?

Sustainable tourism is simply about making a positive difference to the people and environment of destinations we travel to:

Buying local produce can help support communities

What can holidaymakers do?

Just little things can make a big difference at destinations. For example:
⇨ buying locally made souvenirs or crafts;
⇨ eating at local bars and cafes;

⇨ Respecting local cultures and the natural environment.
⇨ Recognising that water and energy are precious resources that we need to use carefully.
⇨ Helping to protect endangered wildlife and preserve the natural and cultural heritage of the places we visit.
⇨ Protecting and enhancing favourite destinations for the future enjoyment of visitors and the people who live there.
⇨ Buying local – giving fair economic returns to local families.
⇨ Enjoying ourselves and taking responsibility for our actions.

⇨ going out on excursions that use local guides and drivers;
⇨ getting around on public transport, bicycles or even walking when possible;
⇨ taking quick showers instead of baths;
⇨ asking not to have towels and sheets replaced on a daily basis;
⇨ not buying products made from endangered plants or wild animals (including hardwoods, corals, shells, starfish, ivory, fur, feathers, skins, horn, teeth, eggs, reptiles and turtles);
⇨ consider compensating for the environmental impact of your flight. Ask your tour operator if they are part of any carbon offset scheme.

Just some of the simple things that can be done – there are many more! Find out in our range of Insider Guides at www.thetravelfoundation. org.uk – 'What you can do'.

You can also ask your tour operator what they are doing to make sure local people can benefit from your visit – and how they are minimising the environmental impact of your visit. They may also be able to offer you the option to make a small donation to the Travel Foundation when you book your holiday, which will help us to continue this important work.

Anyone who takes a holiday can make a positive difference when they travel

You can also text 'donate' to 61199, which will give £2 instantly to help us do more.

Travel that makes a world of difference

With the increasing debate over climate change and the drive to reduce carbon emissions, sustainable tourism gives us an opportunity to make a positive difference when we travel. By doing simple things, we can help ensure that we protect the natural environment and offer maximum benefit to the communities who live in the places we all love to visit.

The Travel Foundation partners with UK travel companies in order to make tourism a force for good – minimising any negative effects on the environment and using income from tourism to help protect precious natural resources. We also encourage the industry to buy goods and services from the local area. This decreases the need for imports (and the many miles these can travel) and allows families living in destinations to earn a better living out of tourism.

Just some of the people we've already been able to help...

Orwin is making a better living for him and his family by selling fresh, local produce to hotels... and giving visitors the real taste of the Caribbean! This is reducing imports and helping the environment.

Ana Lilia is helping to protect cenotes – underground rivers and pools that you can snorkel and dive in – and a precious source of water for visitors and local families. Protecting life and tourism into the future... and offering visitors a truly unique experience of Mexico!

Maria is opening a cafe because of a new excursion taking visitors into the heart of Cyprus – keeping life in the traditional villages... and giving visitors a whole new experience of an old favourite.

Kamala is learning lace making, to sell souvenirs to visitors in Sri Lanka. This is helping to rebuild her life after the tsunami, keeping traditional skills alive and giving visitors the chance to buy real local crafts.

These stories are just the beginning. We are working with the UK travel industry to develop similar practices at destinations across the world. For example, Orwin's experience is helping us to encourage other tour operators and hotels to source local food for their customers. Developing the new excursion in Cyprus, where Maria has opened her cafe, has led to the development of a written guide to help travel companies create more sustainable excursions for their customers to enjoy, giving travellers a richer experience of their chosen destination.

This is great news as it means that what we do has wide impact – it is already changing the way travel companies do business and allowing travellers to make a real difference to the people and places they love to visit.

The Travel Foundation is a UK charity that cares for the places we love to visit

Anyone who takes a holiday can make a positive difference when they travel. Sustainable travel isn't about specialist or 'eco' holidays, it's for every person who takes a holiday... and it can make a huge difference at favourite destinations.

It can help protect the natural environment, traditions and culture – the things that make holidays special. And it can improve the well-being of destination communities – ensuring that local people benefit from tourism and are happy to give visitors a warm welcome.

All of which can give us an even better holiday experience. As well as helping to ensure there are great places for us all to visit – for generations to come!

Responsible, sustainable, green, eco, ethical tourism... all these terms mean pretty much the same thing – holidays that benefit the people and environment in destinations.

Make a world of difference

The Travel Foundation is a UK charity that cares for the people and places we love to visit. It is helping the travel industry take effective action on sustainable tourism, in mainstream destinations across the world. Improving quality and keeping holidays special... into the future.

Holidaymakers and travel companies can find out much more by visiting www.thetravelfoundation. org.uk.

The UK is taking a lead in changing the way the world travels.

⇨ The above information is reprinted with kind permission from the Travel Foundation. Visit www. thetravelfoundation.org.uk for more information.

© The Travel Foundation

What is ecotourism?

Information from i-to-i

The concept of ecotourism is one of ambiguity and dispute. There is no universal definition for ecotourism, nor is there a certifying agency. A common misconception is that ecotourism is just nature-based tourism, the act of surrounding yourself with nature's little wonders. The truth is far more complex. Ecotourism has to be both ecologically and socially conscious. Its goal is to minimise the impact that tourism has on an area through cooperation and management and in some case it even encourages travellers to have a positive impact on their new surroundings.

A commonly accepted definition of ecotourism is:

'Responsible travel to natural areas that conserves the environment and improves the well-being of local people.'*

Ideally, ecotourism should...

⇨ Minimise the negative impacts of tourism.

⇨ Contribute to conservation efforts.

⇨ Employ locally and give money back to the community.

⇨ Educate visitors about the local environment and culture.

⇨ Cooperate with local people to manage natural areas.

⇨ Provide a positive experience for both visitor and host.

Eco-lodges

A hotel that is truly an 'eco-lodge' is one that makes efforts to conserve resources and limit waste. Some things a hotel can do to limit its environmental impact are:

⇨ Reducing temperatures for laundry water.

⇨ Changing sheets and towels less frequently.

⇨ Using solar power or alternative energy sources.

⇨ Installing low flow showerheads and toilets.

⇨ Buying recycled products and recycling waste.

⇨ Building a compost heap or a waste treatment facility.

Many hotels are keen to conserve energy because it both makes them look good and saves them a lot of money. Hotels that are sustainable also contribute to the local community. They buy local food products and hire local employees.

Greenwashing

With ecotourism being so popular, it is inevitable that many companies will claim to be environmentally friendly to get business. This is called greenwashing. Since there is no single certifying agency to determine who actually engages in ecotourism, it is easy to get away with just throwing the term around.

Many hotels claim to be eco-lodges simply because they have a good view. Wildlife viewing trips are often labelled eco-tours even if they give nothing back to local ecology and sometimes cause significant problems to the area's wildlife. Just because something is in nature doesn't make it ecotourism. It's important to look more carefully at their practices to see if it really is ecotourism.

Homestays

A popular alternative to eco-lodges, especially for those who are travelling with a volunteer travel provider such as i-to-i, is to stay in homestay accommodation. The main benefit of this is that your accommodation costs will be going straight back into the community. In many cases your meals are also included and this usually means that local suppliers will benefit from your stay too.

Sustainable, alternative, responsible tourism – what does it all mean?

There are many other words to describe a similar idea. The terms ecotourism, sustainable tourism or responsible tourism are often used interchangeably. The main ideas behind these are all similar, but there are small differences.

Alternative tourism is any type of travel that is not mass tourism (i.e. beach vacations or traditional sightseeing tours). This includes ecotourism, backpacking, volunteer tourism, adventure tourism, historical tourism, tornado chasing, couch surfing or any other form of travel that is atypical.

The widely accepted definition for sustainable tourism is: 'Tourism that meets the needs of present tourists and host regions while protecting and enhancing opportunities for the future.'* It has the same ideals as ecotourism but is not limited to natural areas.

An eco-lodge

Responsible travel is a practice used by travellers guiding how they act in a host country. It has roots in sustainable tourism but focuses on being respectful as a guest in a foreign country, such as asking permission to take photographs or enter a home, observing some of the customs, such as dress, or making an effort to learn the language.

*The International Ecotourism Society (TIES)

⇨ The above information is reprinted with kind permission from i-to-i. Visit www.i-to-i.com for more information.

© i-to-i

Climate change and tourism

Tourism industry leaders pledge to rapidly respond to climate change

DAVOS, Switzerland (Thomson Financial) – Tourism chiefs and UN agencies today pledged to 'green' the travel trade while highlighting the 880bn US$ industry's own vulnerability to global warming.

In a four-page declaration, UN tourism, environment and weather agencies, national tourism officials and executives from 100 countries agreed the industry must 'rapidly respond to climate change' and take 'concrete measures' to curb greenhouse gas emissions.

They also said at the end of a three-day UN conference on tourism and global warming that tourists should be encouraged to consider the environmental impact of their travel choices and reduce their 'carbon footprint'.

The declaration will be put to a ministerial meeting in London on 13 November, officials said.

'The immediate risk is that tourism is demonised for its carbon footprint and regulated because the industry doesn't act to regulate itself,' said Christopher Rodrigues, chairman of the VisitBritain tourism board.

Tourism accounts for up to 6% of global carbon dioxide emissions, according to a UN report in Davos, and the number of travellers is due to more than double by 2020.

Air transport currently accounts for about 40% of these industry emissions, followed by car travel on 32% and accommodation 21%.

Yesterday, an EU parliamentary committee called for controversial carbon emission trading rules on all flights in and out of Europe to be introduced in 2010, earlier than planned.

Andreas Fischlin, a leading scientist on the UN's International Panel on Climate Change (IPCC), told the meeting in Davos that 25 to 40% of all greenhouse gas emissions behind climate change needed to be cut by 2020.

'Tourism has to contribute to mitigation: it's a cause of the problem and has to take up its share,' Fischlin said, warning that some warming was already inevitable.

The tourism industry must 'rapidly respond to climate change'

The measures advocated by the conference included greater energy efficiency, use of renewable energy, better conservation of natural areas to serve as 'earth lungs', technological or design measures to avoid pollution, and staff education on climate change.

IPCC reports released earlier this year underlined that tropical cyclones, storm surges, temperature shifts, and changes in rain and snowfall are already harming tourism in some cases.

The UN World Tourism Organisation predicted this week that climate change would trigger 'very large' shifts in travel habits around the world.

In Davos, island states, beach holiday and winter destinations stressed their concerns about shifts in weather patterns, rising sea levels and declining snow cover that in some instances were eating away at their greatest economic asset.

'What's the main image used to promote a tourist destination? It's a nice landscape,' a UNWTO official pointed out.

Several vulnerable tourist destinations, especially tropical islands like the Maldives and Seychelles, urged greater efforts to curb emissions but also voiced concern about possible restrictions or big taxes on long-haul air travel.

The declaration underlined that new tourism policies must reflect a combination of environmental, climate change, social and economic needs.

3 October 2007

⇨ The above information is reprinted with kind permission from Thomson Financial. Visit their website at www.thomson.com/solutions/financial for more.

© *Thomson Financial*

Aviation's impact on the climate

Quick fixes could cut aviation's impact on climate change, says report

Aviation's role in climate change could be reduced easily by eliminating needless emissions and enabling consumers to make informed choices about how to travel, says a report published today by the International Institute for Environment and Development (IIED) in association with the International Centre for Responsible Tourism.

The report, which IIED commissioned from the Carbon Consultancy, will be launched at the travel sector's annual World Travel Market exhibition in London to mark World Responsible Tourism Day (14 November).

It says that all who benefit from aviation have a collective responsibility for reducing emissions, highlights avoidable greenhouse-gas emissions, and recommends ways to reduce the sector's contribution to climate change quickly and easily.

Topping the list is a call for real and standardised reporting of airline emissions and eco-labelling of flights.

'The statistics surrounding aviation emissions are confusing for consumers because they are based upon a wide variety of source material,' says the report's author, Hugo Kimber of the Carbon Consultancy. 'Even individual flight emissions calculations can vary by as much as 300% for the same flight depending on the methods used.'

The report calls for standard fuel-use reporting by airlines to allow the creation of a flight-labelling scheme. This would help consumers to choose routes and airlines that emit less, which in turn would encourage airlines to adopt more efficient technology and aircraft deployment.

The report adds that more than 20% of aviation capacity flies empty, that indirect flights can emit up

iied

International

Institute for

Environment and

Development

to 29% more carbon dioxide than direct ones, and that the use of aircraft by individual airlines can make a big difference to emissions. But passengers are left in the dark about these figures and so can't exercise consumer power to reduce emissions.

'The environmental impact of aviation is often considered in relation to global emissions, but consumers want to know what the impact of their flight choice will be using standard reporting guideline', says Kimber. 'It is important to enable flight purchasing based upon efficiency but you can't do that without labelling, and for that you need to know how much fuel each airline/aircraft uses in relation to passengers and cargo.'

'Flying produces considerable global benefits, especially for developing countries but at an environmental cost which it must be assessed against by consumers and policymakers,' adds Kimber.

'Our analysis shows that it should be possible for government, consumers and business to make some short-term impacts on emissions reduction via eco labelling, information delivery and to start reflecting the environmental cost in ticket prices.'

One quick fix would be to reduce the baggage allowance. A 5-kilogram reduction in baggage allowance on the main short-haul route from London to Spain would reduce carbon dioxide emissions by 54,400 to 68,000 tonnes – the higher value equating to 2,950 flights from London to Malaga.

The report calls for emissions from aviation to be included in the European carbon-trading system with an interim efficiency-based eco-tax to reflect the cost of carbon. It urges European governments to adopt the proposed Single European Sky – a regional air traffic control system that would eliminate the annual 12 million tonnes of needless carbon dioxide emissions created by national systems.

It says airport expansion should only take place if demand for flying is still rising after passengers and airlines start to bear its environmental cost in line with recommendations already made to the UK government.

'Aviation brings benefits to governments, the public, business and the airlines themselves but nobody is covering the environmental costs,' says Dilys Roe, the senior researcher at IIED who commissioned the study. She points out that air travel is extremely important to the economies of poor countries, both in terms of bringing tourist revenue and exporting fresh produce, so it is key that emission reduction policies do not harm the poor.

'Cutting emissions from aviation is everyone's responsibility and in everyone's interests – make it your responsibility too,' says Harold Goodwin of the International Centre for Responsible Tourism at Leeds Metropolitan University. 'This report shows sensible ways to do this in a way that does not harm those who have contributed least to the problem and will suffer most from its impacts.'
14 November 2007

⇨ The above information is reprinted with kind permission from the International Institute for Environment and Development. Visit www.iied.org for more information.
© *IIED*

Nature's 'doom' is tourist boom

Global warming has led to a new travel boom as holidaymakers embrace what tour operators are calling doomsday tourism – the urge to see some of the world's most endangered sites before they disappear for ever.

By Tim Shipman in Washington

Newly awakened to the perils facing the planet, American tourists are leading the charge to the melting glaciers of Alaska, Patagonia, the Arctic and Antarctic, the sinking islands of the Pacific and the fading glories of the Great Barrier Reef – and their British counterparts are not far behind.

Ken Shapiro, the editor of *TravelAge West*, a magazine for travel agents, said the phenomenon was one of the most significant trends in travel this year. He added: 'I called it the tourism of doom and I got a lot of responses from people in the travel industry.

'Many people are picking a holiday destination because it is threatened or endangered by environmental circumstances. We're hearing it from tour operators and travel agents.'

So far even the more aggressive US travel industry has not marketed sights explicitly as 'doomsday' must-sees. But Mr Shapiro said it was different behind the scenes. 'They may not put it in the brochure, but they say, "See it before it's gone" when talking to customers.'

Dennis and Stacie Woods, from Seattle, revealed last week that they had been choosing holiday destinations based on the level of environmental threat they faced. They have climbed the 19,340ft Mt Kilimanjaro, where scientists say the peak snows could be gone within 15 years. Some 10,000 tourists now climb the Tanzanian mountain every year.

The Woods have also travelled to the Amazon and kayaked around the Galapagos Islands. 'We wanted to see the islands this year,' said Mr Woods, a lawyer, 'because we figured they're only going to get worse.'

The polar icecaps, which some scientists say are melting quickly, are also attracting record numbers of visitors.

According to the International Association of Antarctic Tour Operators, more than 37,000 tourists visited the continent last year – double the number five years ago. A third came from America, while the second largest contingent – one in seven visitors – travelled from Britain. 'There definitely is a rush to see and explore the world before it changes,' said Matt Kareus, of Natural Habitat, which operates excursions to Antarctica.

Quark Expeditions, a company that runs Arctic and Antarctic tours, is doubling its capacity and opening up new routes, including one to the Norwegian Arctic island of Spitsbergen.

Prisca Campbell, Quark's spokesman, said: 'There's not enough capacity to satisfy demand. We always get the question about global warming. There are many folks who are really concerned. Most of our American travellers look at the world and say, "What's left?"'

The publicity garnered by former US vice-president Al Gore, who won both the Nobel Peace Prize and an Oscar for *An Inconvenient Truth*, his 2006 film about global warming, has contributed to an interest in doomsday tourism in America.

'I have just been to the US tour operators' annual conference in Cancun,' said Mr Shapiro. 'Last year, when there was talk about green tourism, people said it was a fad. This year every tour operator is doing it.'

Critics say the rush to 'see it before it's gone' is hastening damage to the environment, encouraging tourists to take flights and other means of travel that contribute to greenhouse gas emissions.

A spokesman for the Will Steger Foundation, a conservation group in Minnesota, said: 'It's hard to fault somebody who wants to see something before it disappears, but it's unfortunate that in their pursuit of doing that, they contribute to the problem.'

But Quark, which takes 7,000 passengers a season to the Arctic and Antarctic, said a survey of its customers this year found that six out of 10 claimed their experiences had 'motivated me to help protect environmentally sensitive areas'.

Miss Campbell added: 'Our philosophy is that you must protect the environment but you must make sure that people get to see it, because if you don't see it, you won't value it. People who travel to these areas are keen to help fight global warming. They go home and tell their friends they've got to do something.'

23 December 2007

Forget the carbon footprint, we want our summer sun

Tiscali Summer Lifestyle Report 2007 reveals Brits won't let global warming get in the way of their summer holiday

The first Summer Lifestyle Report conducted by broadband, telephone and media company Tiscali shows that Brits are far from concerned about their carbon footprint this summer. A massive 67% of Brits admitted that they won't even be thinking about the impact their summer holiday could have on the environment.

US, Australia and Maldives are Brits' dream destinations. The trend is only set to get worse. In 2007 we may be holidaying in Spain (24%), France (11%) or Greece (10%), but we aspire to long-haul destinations. 16% of respondents said their dream holiday would be to the USA, Australia (15%) and the Maldives (13%). The carbon footprint doesn't even register on the scale of our biggest holiday worries; what bothers us most is the possibility that our accommodation won't live up to scratch (28%) or that we might lose our luggage (26%).

What is clear is that we are chasing the sun in even greater numbers. 90% of us choose a more southerly destination, for a Brit sunshine inevitably meaning a flight to warmer climes. Only 4% would consider booking a holiday in the UK in the next 12 months, despite the fact that 54% of us remember childhood holidays in the UK.

Back at home we are also adopting a laid-back 'continental' lifestyle. When asked to describe what summer means to you, replies overwhelmingly favoured barbecues and parties (31%), along with traditional day trips (20%) and gardening (17%). Two-thirds of us will be drinking alcohol at the barbecue but an equal number favoured water and beer as the top summer coolers.

Alex Hole, Tiscali's Online Media Director, says: 'A lot of people were brought up on day trips and summer holidays in Rhyl, Blackpool or Brighton – Britain's traditional summer resorts. But now lower flight costs and last-minute breaks are encouraging us to go for guaranteed sunshine and even exotic holidays. The government's new carbon calculator might get people checking out the carbon cost of their holiday but it's obviously not putting the Brits off their favourite sunny destinations.'

Additional facts

Beachwear – women are bolder on the beach. Half of women will be wearing a bikini on the beach (49%) while only 6% of men opted for Speedos (57% choosing long shorts).

Families and couples dominate holidays – 41% are holidaying with their partner and 44% with their family.

Canadian tourist board pull your socks up! While the vast majority of respondents aspired to go 'somewhere luxurious or exotic' (34%) USA topped the aspirational destination poll as the top specified destination (15%) while only 1% chose neighbours Canada.

Tiscali's new-look travel channel is available at www.tiscali.co.uk/travel where you can book your last-minute deals, shop for your holiday wardrobe and check out Tiscali's travel guides. *18 July 2007*

⇨ Information from Tiscali. Visit www.tiscali.co.uk for more.
© *Tiscali*

Climate change could bring tourists to UK – report

Climate change could 'dramatically' change the face of British tourism in the next 20 years, with European tourists flocking to the UK to escape unbearably hot continental summers, experts say.

Research shows that European tourists may choose to holiday in Britain as resorts nearer to home become too hot.

Weather changes may provide revival opportunities for northern seaside towns such as Blackpool and put new strains on roads and development in southern coastal resorts, a study in the Journal of Sustainable Tourism said.

Academic David Viner, a researcher at the University of East Anglia's Climatic Research Unit in Norwich, produced the report after analysing the work of experts around the globe.

'The likelihood [is] that Mediterranean summers may be too hot for tourists after 2020, as a result of too much heat and water shortages,' the study said.

There were 'opportunities for the revival of northern European resorts, including Blackpool, in the next 20 years, as climate change and rising transport costs offer new holiday opportunities,' it said.

The study added: 'Climate change will impact on many holiday destinations. For many this will be problematic, for others it will produce benefits.'
28 July 2006

© *Guardian Newspapers Limited 2006*

Lord, make us green tourists – but not just yet

Information from the Economic and Social Research Council

If you want to feel guilty about your carbon footprint there is no easier way than taking a cheap flight to the Med for a weekend of sun. Many of us are uneasy about our contribution to global warming and, it seems, would be prepared to reduce our flying to help the planet. Dig a little deeper, however, and the reality is rather different. The evidence is that we are still addicted to 'getting away from it all' – and fast – as Tim Jackson reports.

A few months ago, the BBC launched a web-discussion: 'Would you give up flying for the environment?' Within minutes the site was besieged with respondents. Three days later, I downloaded 350 plus pages of close-typed commentary from well over 2,000 respondents. Forget clunky focus groups, socially desirable responding, and the drip-drip return rates from difficult-to-analyse questionnaires. This stuff is a goldmine.

So what does it tell us? First of all, it reveals just how hot a topic holiday flights have now become. True, we've been blessed with the dubious promise of 'sustainable tourism' for over a decade. In 1997 the frankly disingenuous Berlin Declaration, 'aware that tourism is an important source of economic wealth and one of the fastest growing sectors in the world economy', suggested weakly that: 'tourism activities which directly or indirectly contribute to the conservation of nature and biological diversity and which benefit local communities should be promoted by all stakeholders'.

But to be brutally honest, most of what passes for eco-tourism is still either a niche market for the fit and furiously-committed, or a way of selling increased access to ever more secluded parts of the planet: part of the problem rather than part of the solution. The galloping mainstream

By Tim Jackson

has, until now, sped on regardless. Cheap flights – subsidised by high-price business seats – have given more and more of us access to a myriad sun-kissed destinations. Sustainable tourism remains pretty much an oxymoron.

Sustainable tourism remains pretty much an oxymoron

Now it appears things might be changing. Some at least of the BBC's respondents, seeking carbon forgiveness, insist they already vacation sensibly on the Cornish Riviera. Or perhaps – like me – stack up years of filial resentment by hauling their tweenies up mountains in the Lake District. If you must go abroad for your hols, claim others, why not try 'slow travel'? Hour upon hour of juddering train across the plains of Northern France before you find anywhere remotely interesting. 'But think of all the reading you can do!'

Yes, looking through some of this stuff you could almost believe that the girl next door is finally more interested in the size of your carbon footprint than she is in the size of your Caribbean holiday. And that must be good news for climate change. Mustn't it?

Not quite. A closer look reveals a small but equally vociferous tribe who see the whole thing as the latest foray in a never-ending class war. 'Those rich bastards have had their fun,' the argument goes. 'Now they want to stop us having any.' And to be fair, this moralistic claim has more than a grain of truth in it. The C1s and C2s have done a fair amount of catching up in recent years, but long-distance leisure travel is still skewed in favour of the ABs and the poor old DEs barely get a look in (see chart over page). All the same, I have my suspicions this vociferous defence of the freedom to fly is bandied about as much by those who drive their 4x4s through the rugged terrain of Chelsea as by those who have no choice but to travel on the bus. 'A man beyond the age of 26 who finds himself on a bus can count himself a failure,' claimed Margaret Thatcher, 25 years ago. It became a pernicious and self-fulfilling

Is sustainable air travel really possible?

prophecy. Mobility is the new class. Getting away means getting on.

Most of what passes for eco-tourism is still either a niche market for the fit and furiously-committed, or a way of selling increased access to ever more secluded parts of the planet

---

Never mind that the flight was crowded; the sun lotion ineffective, the ocean murky with algal blooms from too much pressure on the local sewage system. It's the memories that count. These photographs. This illegal relic from Carthage. That curious moment of priceless peace one evening on the beach, kids in the crèche, spouse in the bar, when a midriff cuckoo, draped in chiffon, actually smiled at you. And the sun sank serenely into an azure sea. The having-been-there-ness of it all: that's what I'm clinging to.

At a recent Citizens' Summit on Climate Change, organised by the Department for Environment, Food and Rural Affairs, participants were asked to discuss a variety of simple carbon-saving actions. Easy things that ordinary people could do to reduce their carbon footprint. One group, looking at tourism, argued that the Government should offer tax breaks to those prepared to holiday close to home. Not a bad idea. As everyone knows, five days in Plymouth can cost you as much as 14 nights in Bali.

Secretary of State David Miliband (who, it turns out, is rather good at this engagement stuff) was vaguely amused. 'But how would we know they'd really been to Blackpool and not snuck off to Biarritz?' he mused. (It could be a whole new take on benefit fraud.) 'Easy!' responded some bright spark. 'Just check their suntans.' The whole room laughed. Those who can, holiday abroad; those who can't shiver in Lyme Regis.

Maybe it's the suntan. Maybe it's the azure sea and the chiffon wrap. Maybe it's a deep-rooted quest for authenticity and the mind-broadening propensity of travel (although the desperate hunt for 'British food' by vaguely bilious tourists in Barcelona somehow belies this). At any rate, one thing seems clear: 'getting away' won't be given up so easily. So either we'll have to find somewhere else to go (space travel, anyone?). Or else perhaps it's time to find out what we're all so desperate to get away from.

Summer 2007

⇨ The above information is reprinted with kind permission from the Economic and Social Research Council and is taken from issue 25 of their publication *The Edge*. Visit www.esrc.ac.uk for more information.

© ESRC

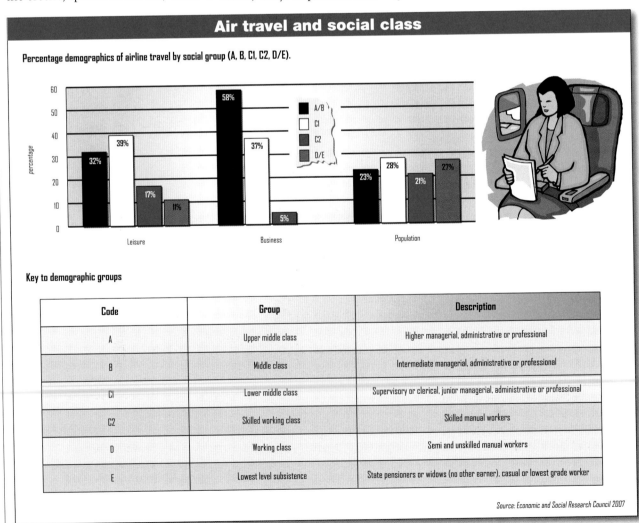

Air travel and social class

Percentage demographics of airline travel by social group (A, B, C1, C2, D/E).

Key to demographic groups

Code	Group	Description
A	Upper middle class	Higher managerial, administrative or professional
B	Middle class	Intermediate managerial, administrative or professional
C1	Lower middle class	Supervisory or clerical, junior managerial, administrative or professional
C2	Skilled working class	Skilled manual workers
D	Working class	Semi and unskilled manual workers
E	Lowest level subsistence	State pensioners or widows (no other earner), casual or lowest grade worker

Source: Economic and Social Research Council 2007

British tourists amongst worst in the world

New research reveals extent of Brits' noisy habits and bad behaviour abroad

The reputation of British tourists abroad remains almost as bad as it was five years ago, according to Expedia's 2007 Best Tourist League. Although Brits are no longer considered 'the worst tourists in the world', they remain in the league's top five, thanks to their noisy and untidy holiday habits, bad behaviour and miserly tipping.

Expedia compiled the 2007 Best Tourist League by asking 15,000 European hoteliers to rank different nationalities according to several key criteria, including behaviour, politeness, tidiness, noise, willingness to speak the local language, holiday spending and fashion sense.

'We decided to compile another Best Tourist League to reassess the reputation of British tourists – obviously with the hope that we would have risen up the ranks since 2002,' says Caroline Cartellieri, managing director of Expedia.co.uk.

'However, it's disappointing to learn that our position in the world rankings hasn't really changed, with foreign hoteliers still perceiving Brits as noisy, untidy and badly dressed. Although it's good to see Brits perceived as generous in their spending habits, now we just need to work on ditching those "socks and sandals".'

Japanese are simply the best

The league reveals the best tourists in the world are the polite and tidy Japanese, who secured 35 per cent more votes than the Americans who came in second. New to this year's list were the Swiss who came in third and were commended for being quiet and considerate. The French took the title of 'World's Worst Tourists' – previously held by the British – due to their unwillingness to speak the local language, lack of generosity and impoliteness.

Hey big spender!

Despite their faults, hoteliers do look favourably upon British spending habits, voting them the third biggest holiday spenders after the Americans and Russians. However, Brits are not so generous when it comes to tipping, with even British hoteliers voting British tourists as the meanest tippers.

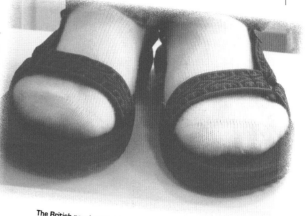

The British penchant for 'socks and sandals' and other holiday fashion disasters appears to be alive and well, with hoteliers voting Brits the second worst dressed tourists

Fashion victims

The British penchant for 'socks and sandals' and other holiday fashion disasters appears to be alive and well, with hoteliers voting Brits the second worst dressed tourists, second only to the Americans. Unsurprisingly, tourists from Italy, France and Spain lead the way in the holiday-style stakes.

Brits...their own worst enemy

British tourists can't even blame cultural differences for their poor performance in the league, with the harshest criticism coming from British hoteliers, who voted them the worst behaved of all nationalities, preferring even the Germans.

Good old British manners also seem to have fallen by the wayside with British hoteliers rating their countrymen the third most impolite nationality. Brits have even shaken off their traditional reserve to become one of the top three biggest holiday complainers.

Key findings

⇨ Overall, the Japanese were voted the World's Best Tourists, followed by the Americans and the Swiss.

⇨ The Japanese were also the best behaved, beating the Germans and the Americans who came top for their behaviour in the 2002 league. The British, Russians and Danes were cited as having the worst behaviour.

⇨ The Americans are no longer the most polite, slipping to third place since 2002. The Japanese are now the most polite while British manners have improved significantly from last place to second this year.

⇨ The Americans have changed their approach to travelling and now rank highest for attempting to speak the local language.

⇨ The Italians are the loudest on holiday followed by the Americans and the British, while the Japanese, Chinese and Swiss are the quietest.'

⇨ Those smooth operators from the Mediterranean are the best dressed with the Italians, French and Spanish coming top in the style stakes.

⇨ The Germans are the perfect guests, tidying up before their chambermaid arrives.

15 May 2007

⇨ The above information is reprinted with kind permission from Expedia. Visit www.expedia.co.uk for more information.

© *Expedia*

Souvenir alert

Information from WWF-UK

You may be tempted to buy wildlife souvenirs on holiday, but remember that trade in many animals, plants and products made them is controlled internationally to safeguard wild species.

Over 800 species of animals and plants are currently banned from international trade and a further 25,000 are strictly controlled by CITES (Convention of International Trade in Endangered Species) and European Union legislation. Those banned from international trade include tigers, rhinos, elephants, whales and marine turtles, and trade is controlled for many corals, reptiles, orchids and cacti.

So think before you buy- you may be breaking the law and your souvenirs could be confiscated by customs on your return.

International trade in the following is prohibited

It is not easy to know which souvenirs or gifts to avoid buying, so here's a brief guide to some you're most likely to come across. International trade is banned altogether. Remember trade exist to protect these animals and plants. Your decisions can help them survive.

Elephant ivory, despite the sanctioning of some legal ivory sales globally, illegal trade in ivory continues and you cannot bring any ivory back to the UK. Watch out for stalls selling ivory carvings and jewellery outside hotels and shops, this occurs particularly in Africa and Asia.

Traditional Asian Medicine containing endangered species. Trade in any medicines claiming to contain species such as tiger, leopard, musk, rhino, bear and plants, such as Sausserea costus, gastrodia orchid or dendrobium orchid, are prohibited.

Sea turtle shells - All jewellery, hair combs and sunglasses made from endangered sea turtles and often found in the Caribbean and tropical beach resorts are banned.

Spotted cat furs - Clothing and curios made from the skins and products of the jaguar, leopard, snow leopard, cheetah and tiger are banned.

Shahtoosh - the wool of the endangered Tibetan Antelope used to make shawls, have become increasingly popular with fashion conscious tourists. However, these products are totally illegal.

International trade in the following requires a special permit

Trade in many plants and animals is controlled so that it does not threaten their survival in the wild. You may bring back souvenirs made from certain species where international trade is allowed, provided they are for your personal use and you have a CITES permit from the country of export.

Live animals and wild birds - regardless of species, all must have health certificates from Defra and go through a quarantine period, before they can legally enter the UK. New legislation means no wild birds can be brought into the UK, with trade only allowed in captive-bred birds from approved countries (Australia, Brazil, Canada, Chile, Croatia, Israel, New Zealand and the USA).

Coral - nearly a million species depend on coral reefs but coral is sold in various forms, such as jewellery and ornaments.

Queen conch shells - these large pink and white shells can be found in the Caribbean Sea, but require a permit for import to the UK.

Orchids and Cacti - the demand for protected specimens of plants continues. These all require permits for import into the UK.

Reptile skin products- Bags, shoes, watch-straps and belts made from the skins of snake, lizard, alligator and crocodile require permits to import. Some live snakes and lizards are also illegally traded as pets!

Caviar - all species of sturgeon and their caviar (unfertilised eggs) are covered by controls. You may however bring up to 125 grams of caviar into the EU for personal consumption.

REMEMBER - If you are unsure about whether you need a permit to import wildlife souvenirs from abroad, check with the UK Department of the Environment Food and Rural Affairs (Defra) before you buy. Call 0117 987 8749 or visit www.defra.gov.uk.

⇨ The above information is reprinted with kind permission from WWF-UK, Souvenir alert leaflet, www.wwf.org.uk/wildlifetrade/buy.asp, August 2007. Visit www.wwf.org.uk for more information.

© WWF-UK

Slum tours: a day trip too far?

A new travel experience gives visitors a glimpse into the harsh lives of Delhi's street children. But is it a worthy initiative or just an example of voyeuristic 'poorism', asks Amelia Gentleman

Clearing his throat theatrically as he gets ready to reveal a highlight of the tour, group leader Javed stops halfway up the staircase to platform one and points through the railings to a dark alcove beneath the footbridge over the tracks.

'This is where the street children sleep,' he says, smiling at the cluster of tourists who are craning forward to hear his voice above the roar of the trains below. A small boy climbs out from the hole, steps across the corrugated iron roof and balances himself on a ledge on the other side of the bars, staring back at the visitors, perplexed.

The tourists pause for a while taking in his malnourished appearance, his filthy clothes and glazed eyes. The boy doesn't say anything, but Javed briskly explains that this child, like a lot of the homeless children who live in New Delhi railway station, is addicted to a white correction fluid, called Eraz-Ex.

Most carry a small square of cloth soaked in the chemical, which they hold to their noses and inhale periodically. 'They spend more than half the money they earn from selling rubbish they find on the platform on buying it from the stationery stalls in the market,' he says. 'It does make them a bit violent.'

He pauses to give the group of visitors from Australia, Russia and England a chance to ask questions, before running through the advantages of sleeping in the gap between the platform roof and the walkway. It's shady and you have to be small to get to it, which makes it relatively safe from the station police. But there are the overhead electricity wires to look out for. 'Several of the children have been electrocuted by that wire,' he adds.

For anyone weary of Mughal tombs and Lutyens architecture, a new tourist attraction is on offer for visitors to the Indian capital: a tour of the living conditions endured by the 2,000 or so street children who live in and around Delhi's main railway stations. For two hours, tour guides, themselves former street children, show visitors what life is like for the city's most deprived inhabitants.

> ## There is something a little uncomfortable about the experience – cheerful visitors in bright holiday T-shirts gazing at profound misery

The money raised (200 rupees a ticket – £2.50) goes to a well-respected local charity which tries to rehabilitate these children. The trip is designed as an awareness-raising venture and organisers deny that this is the latest manifestation of 'poorism' – voyeuristic tourism, where rich foreigners come and gape at the lives of impoverished inhabitants of developing countries. Bus tours of the shanty towns of Soweto or guided walks through the slums of Rio have attracted curious tourists for many years; the visit to Delhi's railway underworld has been running for just a few months but has already proved popular with Western and Indian visitors.

'We've come to educate ourselves about these homeless children who live near us. Most of the time people ignore them; I think it's good to pay them some attention,' an Indian post-graduate student in the group says.

The tour guide instructs visitors not to take pictures (although he makes an exception for the newspaper photographer). 'Sometimes the children don't like having cameras pointed at them, but mostly they are glad that people are interested in them,' Javed claims, adding that the friendly smiles of the tourists are more welcome than the railway policemen's wooden sticks and the revulsion of the train travellers. He hopes the trip will get a listing in the Lonely Planet guides. Nevertheless there is something a little uncomfortable

about the experience – cheerful visitors in bright holiday T-shirts gazing at profound misery.

Next up is the railway medical centre where a queue of half a dozen children is waiting to see a young doctor. Wearily she lists the problems the children face – broken limbs from collision with the trains or from falling off moving carriages as they go about their work gathering discarded plastic water bottles, injuries from the beatings meted out by the station police, malnutrition, tuberculosis.

Organisers deny that this is the latest manifestation of 'poorism' – voyeuristic tourism, where rich foreigners come and gape at the lives of impoverished inhabitants of developing countries

---

'Do you see a lot of unwanted pregnancies?' one tourist asks. 'What kind of accidents do you see?' The questions keep coming. Eventually the doctor points out that she has to give her attention to the boy slumped weakly in front of her desk. 'There are a lot of patients waiting,' she says firmly and the group is ushered out.

The tour moves swiftly on to a secluded train siding, where around 15 children are sitting on a carpet, each with a small blackboard, helped by a volunteer to write a few letters and numbers. These are children who live with their families in the tents and shacks around the station. Their parents have brought them to the capital to escape desperate rural poverty. Protected by their relatives from the harshest violence of street life, these children are better off than the orphans who sleep on the station roof, but life remains a battle against hunger.

This school is run by the Salaam Baalak Trust, which is the organisation behind the tourist trips. There doesn't appear to be much formal teaching going on, but the children seem happy

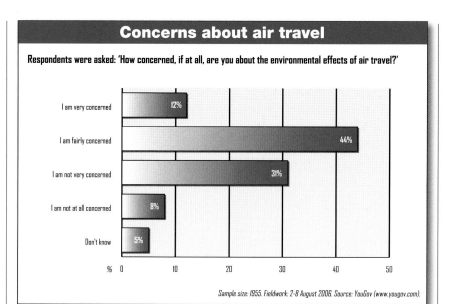

Concerns about air travel

Respondents were asked: 'How concerned, if at all, are you about the environmental effects of air travel?'

I am very concerned	12%
I am fairly concerned	44%
I am not very concerned	31%
I am not at all concerned	8%
Don't know	5%

Sample size: 1955. Fieldwork: 2-8 August 2006. Source: YouGov (www.yougov.com).

to be grouped in this quieter stretch of the station, under adult supervision.

Javed explains how each platform is controlled by a gang leader, one of the older street children, who protects and menaces the other boys in his care. Shouting to make himself heard above the rumbling of the trains, our guide explains that children who run away from home – escaping alcoholism, poverty, natural disasters and family violence – usually take the train to Delhi. Gang leaders spot a new arrival as soon as he steps off the train and offer help with finding food and safe places to sleep.

New arrivals are shown how to strap sharp blades to their index fingers for slashing pockets; they learn which fruit-juice sellers will protect them and where to sell the plastic bottles and silver foil picked from the carriage. Their day's takings are taken by the gang leader who redistributes the money (although not all of it) on Saturday, when the children take a day off to watch Bollywood movies. Platform one, where the luxury tourist trains stop, is the most heavily policed area, but also the most lucrative fiefdom, and street children are skilled at dodging trains to crawl into the carriages from the other side. There are no girls in the gangs because they are picked up by pimps as soon as they arrive, Javed explains.

By the end of the walk, the group is beginning to feel overwhelmed by the smells of hot tar, urine and train oil. Have they found it interesting, Javed asks. One person admits to feeling a little disappointed that they weren't

able to see more children in action – picking up bottles, moving around in gangs. 'It's not like we want to peer at them in the zoo, like animals, but the point of the tour is to experience their lives,' she says. Javed says he will take the suggestion on board for future tours.

To see how the children work the trains, you must arrive just after dawn, when the night trains arrive one after the other, full of discarded junk. Small packs of children, aged between seven and 14, drag huge sacks behind them picking up any litter that can be sold. On a stretch of abandoned track, 100 metres away from the platforms they sort through their findings – snatched purses and half-eaten train meals among the rubbish.

Babloo, who thinks he is 10, has been living here for maybe three years. His hands are splashed white from the correction fluid that he's breathing in through his clenched left fist, and he pulls a dirty bag filled with bottles with his other hand. His life is unrelentingly bleak and he recognises this. 'I don't know why people come and look at us,' he says.

For details of the tours email sbttour@yahoo.com, call Javed on 00 91 98 109 75 284 or see www. salaambaalaktrust.com.

See how the other half lives
Rio de Janeiro
There are 750 favelas in Rio, which are home to 20 per cent of the city's population. While tourists are not advised to wander into these hillside shanty towns unaccompanied,

walking tours of some of the safer neighbourhoods are available, which will give tourists a fascinating insight into favela life. Some of the tours include visits to community projects and health centres. A three-hour tour of the Vila Canoas and Rocinha favelas is available from Favela Tour (00 55 21 33 22 27 27; www.favelatour.com.br).

Soweto

You can stay in a bed and breakfast in the Johannesburg township of Soweto, where nine ethnic groups live peacefully together. The township was featured recently in the film *Tsotsi*, and visitors should see shacks, hospitals and the Nelson Mandela museum, while their money helps to regenerate the area. Day tours plus overnight stay are £95 with the Soweto B&B Association. Trips can be booked as part of longer itineraries with Rainbow Tours (020 7226 1004; www.rainbowtours.co.uk).

New York

The streets of the Bronx and East Harlem districts of NYC are known for high levels of unemployment, crime and a disadvantaged and alienated population. But with their mix of Puerto Ricans, Irish, Italians and Afro-Americans they have also given birth to a rich culture and many important genres of music. A tour traces the area's story through its musical roots. Spots relating to the origins of mambo, ska, soul and hip-hop are included. From around £8 for a couple of hours, details from 00 1 718 542 4139; www.thepoint.org.

Belfast

A driver will offer an in-depth commentary while driving you round the areas of Belfast affected by the Troubles on a Black Taxi Tour (028 9030 1832; www.belfastcityblacktaxitours.com). Shankill and Falls Roads, the peace line dividing the Protestant and Catholic areas, the famous murals and the main city sites are included. It costs £25 for two people.

Rotterdam

About half of Rotterdam's population is from, or has a parent from, outside the Netherlands. Residents will welcome you into their homes, shops, cafes and places of worship on a tour of the deprived ethnic areas, including the predominantly Muslim Spangen. City Safari Tours (010 436 35 67; www.citysafari.nl) arranges tours for £32 per person. These are unguided, but you get a map showing the places to stop and meet the locals.

7 May 2006

⇨ This article first appeared in *The Observer*.

© *Guardian Newspapers Limited 2006*

Murder, genocide and war: the new tourist attractions

Rise in 'dark tourism' as thousands visit death sites

Tourists are showing an increasing appetite for death and disaster as increasing numbers flock to graveyards and killing fields around the world every year.

From the modern-day fascination with Ground Zero in New York to the continuing pull of Auschwitz-Birkenau in Poland and even the Necropolis in Glasgow, 'dark tourism', as it is dubbed, is an industry on the up.

Speaking ahead of a major conference, Professor John Lennon, of Glasgow Caledonian University, said the interest in our recent tragic past is showing little sign of abating. 'People want to go and be tourists in war zones while wars are happening. They seem to have an appetite to get very close while the blood is still dripping. There is no limit to the appetite for this stuff and demand is driving it faster and faster.

'We are always fascinated by the dark side of human nature and the most evil things people can do.'

By David Christie

While around 700,000 people visit the Auschwitz death camps every year, new sites have been adopted by macabre tourists. Lennon notes how hundreds of tourists each day visit Ground Zero, 'trying to remember not to smile as they get their photo taken'. More gruesome sites include the graves of Soham murder victims Holly Wells and Jessica Chapman.

The media and internet are considered key factors in this growth industry, with films such as *Braveheart*, *Schindler's List* and *JFK* boosting their respective death site's

visitor numbers every time they are broadcast, explained Lennon, who will speak on Tuesday at the Dark Tourism Forum conference, organised by the University of Central Lancashire. He will discuss the impact of this industry on Cambodia, where the killing fields of Choeung Ek and interrogation centre Tuol Sleng have emerged as unlikely tourist destinations. Estimates suggest 90% of the near-200,000 annual visitors are foreign tourists.

Tourists are showing an increasing appetite for death and disaster as increasing numbers flock to graveyards and killing fields around the world every year

Some countries, Lennon argues, are undertaking a worryingly selective approach when confronting their past, choosing only to address the glories and ignoring tragedy.

He added: 'In the Czech Republic, the Jewish holocaust is well covered but, by comparison, the genocide of the gypsy people, the Roma, is almost uncommunicated. That is a story that should be told, but people are not banging a gong for it.'

In Scotland, the two most recent tragedies – Lockerbie and Dunblane – were marked with gardens of remembrance and, while some people may prefer to destroy living memories of a tragedy, Lennon argues this isn't necessarily the best solution. He said: 'There is no limit to how low human curiosity can get, but it is a tough call to just destroy buildings.

'For every 10 that go to a site, there will be one that gets interested and learns from it.'

William Black is not convinced. The 26-year-old computer analyst from Paisley visited New York in February 2002 with his girlfriend and found they were the only two people who chose not to hop off the packed double-decker tour bus for a glimpse of Ground Zero.

Black said: 'We felt it was a bit sick. It was five months down the line but they were still pulling bits of bodies from the rubble. The way the tours were marketed seemed wrong, saying "come down and see the destruction al-Qaeda has brought to America".'

'Dark tourism', as it is dubbed, is an industry on the up

Back home, a spokeswoman for VisitScotland said that though they do tap into the many ghosts and monsters that lurk around the country, this is as far as they go. She added: 'We would not brand this dark tourism as these are history-based themes and help raise and stimulate interest in Scotland.'

By 2008 more than 10,000 pupils from across the UK will visit Auschwitz as part of a nationwide educational project organised by the Holocaust Educational Trust (HET).

HET chief executive Karen Pollock said: 'It is going beyond the history textbook. It makes them question further. It also allows them to shape the future by teaching young people to stand up and say something now, not wait till views, policies or actions have become entrenched.'
25 March 2007

⇨ The above information is reprinted with kind permission from the *Sunday Herald*. Visit www.sundayherald.com for more information.

© *Sunday Herald*

Debauchery tourism sets holiday trends

By Rachel Williams

It is a far cry from the civilised city break, relaxing package holiday by the beach, or wholesome trekking trip in the mountains. Inspired by tales of the hedonistic getaways enjoyed by celebrities, the latest fashion for twenty- and thirtysomething holidaymakers is 'debauchery tourism' – or debaucherism – according to a global travel trends report released today.

Hard drinking, gambling and strip clubs are all on the bill as 25- to 34-year-olds embrace the adult version of the American 'spring break' (where college students take to the beaches to party for a week) with a 'work hard, play harder' ethic.

Las Vegas reigns supreme as the US capital of debaucherism, the report for this week's World Travel Market in London said. More hotels are offering pool parties and hiring out individual cabanas with lounge chairs and tables for $1,000 (£478) to $5,000 a day. Long-haul destinations expected to cash in include Buenos Aires and Cape Town. Some cruise companies are offering 24-hour entertainment to younger customers. Market intelligence firm Euromonitor International, which produced the report, said the trend would not be confined to younger travellers.

'Even as travellers age they will continue to embrace travel as an opportunity to revisit their hedonistic youth and to spend lavishly, enjoying their leisure time to the full,' global travel and tourism research manager Clement Wong said.

Another trend predicted to grow substantially was 'diaspora tourism' – immigrants returning to their home countries, often to trace their family roots. The report also said there was untapped potential for 'halal tourism' in the Middle East and suggested an airline could be set up offering halal food, calls for prayer, Qur'ans and separate sections for male and female passengers.
12 November 2007

© *Guardian Newspapers Limited 2007*

Child sex tourism

Information from World Vision UK

Child sex tourism is the commercial sexual exploitation of children by foreigners. It takes place when people travel from their own country to another to intentionally engage in sexual acts with children and when foreigners engage in sexual activity with a child while overseas for some other purpose, for example, on holiday or business.

Child sex tourism is particularly prevalent in situations where women and children experience increased vulnerability to poverty and, therefore, have little economic, social or political status.

Child sex tourism is one of the worst violations of children's rights. This global problem has a huge human cost. The sexual exploitation of children can result in:

⇨ long-lasting physical, social, spiritual, and psychological damage;
⇨ disease (including HIV and AIDS);
⇨ violence/abuse, drug addiction;
⇨ unwanted pregnancy and forced abortions;
⇨ malnutrition;
⇨ social ostracism.

Child sex tourism and the UK

World Vision research has shown that British men are among the top five nationalities to sexually abuse children in Cambodia. Other evidence suggests that they are significant offenders in a number of other known destination countries for child sex tourists.

For this reason, World Vision has been working to:

⇨ raise awareness of the issue with the UK travelling public;
⇨ see better enforcement of existing legislation, which can be used to prevent registered sex offenders travelling from the UK to known destinations, and prosecute British nationals who offend against children overseas;
⇨ promote the need for new legislation to better combat child sex tourism.

World Vision has recently inputted into a Home Office consultation on how to use the Sexual Offences Act 2003 to better effect in efforts to protect children overseas from exploitation and abuse.

Our primary recommendations

⇨ All registered sex offenders (RSOs) should be required to notify of all foreign travel;

This would mean that the UK authorities would know beforehand the travel plans of all registered offenders and, as such, be able to notify the authorities of the country to which the offender will travel. This would allow for greater preventative measures to be taken to ensure that the offender does not offend abroad.

Child sex tourism is one of the worst violations of children's rights. This global problem has a huge human cost

---

Currently, under the Sexual Offences Act 2003 registered sex offenders are required to notify police if they plan to travel outside the UK for more than three days. Case evidence shows that British travellers and expatriates have been involved in the abuse and exploitation of children in places such as Romania and the Czech Republic. Such destinations can be easily visited within a period of three days.

⇨ Extra-territorial law must be used more.

According to extra-territorial law, UK authorities can prosecute for sexual offences convicted overseas against children under 16 by British citizens or residents.

However, since their introduction in 1997, these provisions have only been used to bring four prosecutions, resulting in all of three convictions.

The successful use of extra-territorial laws in the protection of children sends a strong prevention message. Consequently, its use and promotion is essential in combating child sex tourism.

⇨ The dual criminality requirement in extra-territorial law must be removed.

This requires that the offence committed abroad is also required to

be an offence in the national's own country for a prosecution to take place in the UK. Typically child sex tourism occurs in countries where there is a low age of consent – for example, Thailand's and Romania's consensual age is 15 years old, whereas Bulgaria's is just 14.

Child sex tourism is the commercial sexual exploitation of children by foreigners

➪ Foreign travel orders should be used more.

These can restrict the foreign travel of those on the sex offenders' register, therefore minimising the risk to children abroad. However, only one foreign travel order was made in 2004/2005 (Source: Home Office, 2004/5).

This highlights that the authorities are not as proactive as they could be on strategies to prevent the sexual abuse of children overseas by British nationals.

World Vision works with other agencies on these issues, and is a member of ECPAT UK.

What is World Vision doing about child sex tourism?

World Vision has been working on the issue of child sex tourism for a number of years and employs a five-pronged strategy of:

➪ promoting legislation change and enforcement;
➪ deterrence messages in sending and destination countries, which highlight the penalties associated with sexually exploiting children overseas;
➪ law enforcement assistance;
➪ programmes to prevent children from being drawn into the commercial sex trade;
➪ recovery and rehabilitation programmes for children who have been sexually exploited or abused by child sex tourists;
➪ World Vision has succeeded in influencing the UK government on a number of occasions.

➪ The above information is reprinted with kind permission from World Vision UK. Visit www.worldvision.org.uk for more information.

© World Vision UK

Child sex tourism – FAQs

Information from ECPAT

What is the commercial sexual exploitation of children?

It involves the sexual abuse of a child by an adult paid for either by cash or in kind (through meals, clothes, payment of rent etc.). It is also a form of forced labour and a contemporary form of slavery. It includes all acts that are demeaning, degrading and many times life-threatening to children. The three main elements are:

➪ the prostitution of children;
➪ the abuse of children in pornography;

➪ the trafficking of children for sexual exploitation.

However, there are other aspects to the commercial sexual exploitation of children, such as the sexual exploitation of children in tourism, which may incorporate the issue of child prostitution, but could be all three issues.

How many children are affected?

It is impossible to estimate how many children have been affected. The covert and criminal nature of child sex crimes and the vulnerability of children make data collection a difficult task.

It is impossible to estimate how many children have been affected by commercial sexual exploitation

Evidence of child sexual exploitation is primarily anecdotal or in the form of specific case studies. Much of the research and data that exists is not disaggregated by age or gender.

Who are the children and why are they vulnerable?

Many interlinked factors make children, both boys and girls, especially vulnerable to sexual exploitation worldwide. Those most at risk of

What are the consequences for children?

Commercial sexual exploitation denies a child its right to enjoy childhood and to lead a productive, rewarding and dignified life. It can result in serious, even life-threatening consequences for the physical, psychological and social development of children. Children and young people who are victims of sexual exploitation often suffer from physical and sexual abuse, often of an extreme kind, such as rape and torture. The emotional damage is extensive and requires specialist counselling and care. Usually, the longer the exploitation, the more health problems that will be experienced. But some children will suffer life-long damage very quickly, such as contracting AIDS. In addition, many children lose their trust in adults, become anti-social, fearful and anxious. They experience this violence at an age when they should normally be trusting, innocent, healthy and energetic youngsters. The consequences are devastating and affect all aspects of their lives.

abuse include children with little or no education, those who are homeless, orphaned, working on the streets, trafficked, and separated from their families during war or natural disasters, from broken families, children affected by drug and alcohol abuse and those who have already been abused within their family. Children in these circumstances often do not have the confidence, power or opportunity to speak out and thus they become invisible victims.

Persons involved in the commercial sexual exploitation of children may include family members, community leaders, the private sector and organised criminal networks

---

The root causes are complex. Poverty is only one factor. Economic and gender inequality place a large burden on girl children. Social exclusion and lack of education particularly impact on children from marginalised communities and minority ethnic groups. Millions of children have also been orphaned by AIDS. Criminals, including child sex offenders and traffickers, prey on these communities and their children by offering money and hope. Ignorance, lack of education and desperation also lead families to sell their own children.

Who is involved?

A wide range of individuals and groups contribute to the commercial sexual exploitation of children. In addition to the child sex offender, persons involved in the commercial sexual exploitation of children may include family members, community leaders, the private sector and organised criminal networks. Deception is most often used to lure children away from a more protective environment, however, poverty, addiction to drugs and discrimination against girl children and greed are all factors putting children at risk of abuse from their families and communities. Children can also be lured and deceived into the sex industry by former sex workers who promise money and a better life. It is becoming more apparent that organised criminal networks take part in procuring and channelling children toward commercial sexual exploitation and in perpetuating such exploitation.

⇨ The above information is reprinted with kind permission from ECPAT. Visit www.ecpat.org.uk for more information.

© ECPAT

British behaviour abroad

Top 10 countries where British nationals required the most consular assistance (excluding Advice and Self Help cases) from 1 April 2005 to 31 March 2006.

Country	Estimated no. British visits (ONS)	Lost passports	Total arrests	Hospitalisations	Reported rapes	Deaths	Total no. serious assistance cases
Spain	13,795,000	6,078	1,549	601	41	1,325	5,627
USA	4,116,000	3,064	1,368	73	4	125	3,006
Greece	2,443,000	391	226	955	48	139	2,316
France	10,984,000	713	108	210	6	376	1,408
Germany	2,474,000	1,236	210	42	0	284	1,381
Cyprus	1,424,000	333	330	128	10	63	996
India	847,000	144	35	52	0	111	914
Thailand	381,000	653	108	233	5	224	897
Czech Republic	813,000	445	36	52	1	16	845
Australia	650,000	2,023	48	40	1	59	815

Source: 'British behaviour abroad' press release, 2 August 2007, Foreign and Commonwealth Office. www.fco.gov.uk/travel. Crown copyright.

⇨ Nearly 70 million visits abroad were taken by UK residents in 2007. (page 1)

⇨ PriceWaterhouseCoopers reports that the luxury travel market has grown between 8 and 9% a year over the past few years and estimates that it is worth £5 billion in the UK. (page 2)

⇨ There were a record number of tourist and business visits (that is, visits for less than 12 months) both to and from the United Kingdom in 2006, according to a report published today by the Office for National Statistics. (page 3)

⇨ Latest research from Mintel finds that last year alone we went on no less than 205,000 health and wellness holidays, where we benefited from the likes of yoga classes, holistic healing, spa visits or even surgical recuperation. (page 4)

⇨ One in ten (12%) British adults would consider having surgery or an operation abroad because it is cheaper, and as many as a quarter (25%) would be interested in recuperating in a hotel after an illness or operation. (page 5)

⇨ The top holiday fib is the quality of weather abroad, with 9 per cent telling lies about glorious sunshine that did not, in fact, materialise. (page 5)

⇨ The Eiffel Tower and Stonehenge are the tourist 'hotspots' that leave the most Brits cold, according to research by Virgin Travel Insurance that reveals the most disappointing sights at home and abroad. (page 6)

⇨ Online bookings for special interest holidays are booming, according to a report by Travelzest. (page 7)

⇨ In 2006 the UK ranked sixth in the international tourism earnings league behind the USA, Spain, France, Italy and China. (page 8)

⇨ Today's tourists are more likely to 'fly cheap and sleep expensive', travel further for shorter periods and seek out enriching experiences on their holidays, according to Expedia. (page 11)

⇨ Up to 200,000 Britons take a gap year every year, 130,000 of them are school-leavers. (page 19)

⇨ The average gap year traveller spends around £4,800. (page 19)

⇨ There is no doubt that the economies of many impoverished areas of the world have come to benefit hugely from tourism – after all, it is one of the three biggest industries on the planet. (page 21)

⇨ An increase in mass tourism that is not controlled responsibly can ruin areas of natural beauty. Tourism can damage coral reefs, pollute beaches and destroy the habitats of wildlife as roads and hotels are built. Ironically, damage to these natural resources is likely to reduce future numbers of visitors. Another negative effect is that the increasing numbers of aeroplane flights are a major cause of global warming. (page 22)

⇨ The concept of ecotourism is one of ambiguity and dispute. There is no universal definition for ecotourism, nor is there a certifying agency. (page 24)

⇨ Aviation's role in climate change could be reduced easily by eliminating needless emissions and enabling consumers to make informed choices about how to travel, says a report published by the International Institute for Environment and Development. (page 26)

⇨ According to the International Association of Antarctic Tour Operators, more than 37,000 tourists visited the continent last year – double the number five years ago. A third came from America, while the second largest contingent – one in seven visitors – travelled from Britain. (page 27)

⇨ The first Summer Lifestyle Report conducted by Tiscali shows that Brits are far from concerned about their carbon footprint this summer. A massive 67% of Brits admitted that they won't even be thinking about the impact their summer holiday could have on the environment. (page 28)

⇨ Climate change could 'dramatically' change the face of British tourism in the next 20 years, with European tourists flocking to the UK to escape unbearably hot continental summers, experts say. (page 28)

⇨ The reputation of British tourists abroad remains almost as bad as it was five years ago, according to Expedia's 2007 Best Tourist League. Although Brits are no longer considered 'the worst tourists in the world', they remain in the league's top five, thanks to their noisy and untidy holiday habits, bad behaviour and miserly tipping. (page 31)

⇨ 12% of those surveyed by YouGov admitted to being 'very concerned' about the environmental effects of air travel, while a further 44% were 'fairly concerned'. (page 34)

⇨ Tourists are showing an increasing appetite for death and disaster as increasing numbers flock to graveyards and killing fields around the world every year. (page 35)

⇨ British men are among the top five nationalities to sexually abuse children in Cambodia. (page 37)

Carbon footprint

Your carbon footprint is a calculation of the impact you have on the environment. It is based on the amount of greenhouse gases which are produced by your activities and measured in units of carbon dioxide. Reducing air travel is one way of cutting down your carbon footprint, as the increasing number of flights taken is a major cause of climate change.

Child sex tourism

The abuse and commercial exploitation of children which occurs when foreigners travel abroad to engage in sexual activity with a child. Children who live in poverty are particularly vulnerable to child sex tourism, which can include prostitution, trafficking and the abuse of children through pornography.

Colonialism

Colonialism refers to one country governing and controlling another. In the past, wealthy countries have expanded their territory by claiming other countries as their property, causing the weaker country to become dependent on them. Colonialism is often associated with Britain's imperial past, and some critics of gap years have argued that they are a new form of colonialism.

'Dark tourism'

A term coined to describe the trend for visiting sites notorious for death, suffering and tragedy, such as Auschwitz death camp where the Nazis murdered millions during the Holocaust, and Ground Zero in New York (the site where the World Trade Centre stood before the events of 11 September 2001).

Debauchery

Excessive indulgence in pleasure, sometimes of an illegal, immoral or irresponsible nature.

'Doomsday tourism'

A term coined to describe the new trend for visiting endangered areas which are under environmental threat before they disappear forever. Destinations such as the polar icecaps, which are at risk due to the effects of climate change, are receiving an increasing number of visitors each year. However, this only contributes further to the degradation of the area, speeding its destruction.

Ecotourism

A form of responsible travel to a natural area, when the tourist is committed to conserving the environment and improving the lives of local people.

Gap year

A period spent travelling, volunteering or working abroad, typically taken by students for a year between leaving secondary school and starting university, or between leaving university and entering employment.

Medical tourism

Travelling abroad to undertake medical treatment because a procedure is cheaper or more readily available, or sometimes because the medical procedure is not allowed by law in one's own country (for example, women from Ireland may travel to the UK if they wish to have an abortion). Medical tourism is a growing trend, with many people choosing to go abroad for operations, dental procedures or cosmetic surgery.

Package holiday

A trip arranged by a travel agent, in which travel, accommodation and food are all arranged and included in the price.

Slum

An overcrowded and run-down residential area in a city, where people live in poor housing in poverty.

Sustainable tourism

Sustainable or responsible tourism minimises the negative impacts of tourism through an awareness of cultural expectations, respect for local customs, support of local businesses and protection of the environment. Sustainable tourism benefits the community and country and ensures the area is preserved for the future.

Tourism

Tourism is generally defined as travel for the purposes of recreation or leisure for a period of less than a year. Tourism is one of the largest global industries and a vital source of income for many countries, but there are also many ethical and environmental problems associated with it. These include concerns about climate change caused by air travel, destruction of local communities and economies, erosion of beauty spots and exploitation of local workers.

'Voluntourism'

The term 'voluntourism' or 'charity tourism' refers to the growing trend of combining a trip abroad with volunteer work. Volunteering abroad can be a rewarding experience for the traveller and local communities, but there are a growing number of organisations that arrange volunteer placements in developing countries at a high price and with little benefit to the host country.

INDEX

accommodation statistics 8, 11
air travel 3, 21
    environmental impact 21, 26
airport security and congestion 1
alternative tourism 24
Ansari, Anousheh
Apollo 13 12

Bath 9
Belfast, tours 35
Birmingham 9-10
Bournemouth 10
Bradford 10
Branson, Richard 12
Brighton 10
Bristol 10
British identity 9
British men and child sex tourism 37

Cambridge 10
carbon dioxide emissions, tourism 25
carbon offsetting 1
Cardiff 10
child sex tourism 37-9
climate change
    and British tourism 28
    and tourism 1, 25
    tourist attitudes to 28-30
commercial sexual exploitation of children 38-9
cruising 1-2
culture, effects of tourism 22

dark tourism 35-6
death sites as tourist venues 35-6
debauchery tourism 36
dependency on tourism 21
designer holidays 2
diaspora tourism 36
diversity, Britain 9
domestic tourism 8
doomsday tourism 27

Easyjet 11
eco-lodges 24
ecotourism 20, 24
Edinburgh 10
employment, tourism industry 10
environmental concerns, effect on holiday plans 28-30
environmental damage as tourist attraction 27
environmental impact of tourism 20, 21, 22, 25
    air travel 26
    reducing 24
exchange rate, effect on tourism 1
experiential holidays 2

ferry travel 2

gap years 15-19
Glasgow 10
greenhouse gas emissions, reducing 25
greenwashing 24
ground handlers 9

halal tourism 36
Hawking, Stephen 12
health and wellness holidays 4-5
holiday destinations 3
holiday plans, effects of climate change 28-30
holidays as status symbols 5
homestays 24
hotels, limiting environmental impact 24

illegal wildlife trade souvenirs 32
inbound tourism to the UK 3-4, 8
India, street children as tourist sights 33-4
inequality, effects of tourism 20
Internet and travel industry 1

Leeds 10
local economy, effects of tourism 22
London 10
luxury holidays 2

Manchester 10
mass tourism, effects 22
medical tourism 4-5
multiculturalism, Britain 9
must-see tourist sights 6

New York, tours of deprived areas 35
Newcastle 10
Newquay 10
niche travel 7
Nottingham 10

online booking 1
overseas visitors to UK 3-4, 8

poorism 33-5

registered sex offenders, travel restriction 37
responsible travel 1, 20-39
    definition 24
Rio de Janeiro, shanty town tours 34-5
Rotterdam, tours of deprived areas 35
round-the-world tickets 15
Ryanair 11

sex offenders, travel restrictions 37
sexual exploitation of children 38-9

Sherwood Forest 10
short breaks 2
slum tours 33-5
'smart travellers' 11
souvenirs, wildlife 32
Soweto township tours 35
space tourism 12-14
SpaceShipOne 13
SpaceShipTwo 13
spa holidays 5
special interest holidays 7
spending on tourism 5, 8
street children as tourist sights 33-4
'superbreaks' 11
sustainable tourism 22-3, 24
  attitudes to 29-30
Swansea 10

threatened environments as tourist destinations 27
Tito, Dennis 12, 13
tour operators 1
tourism
  and climate change 1, 25, 28-30
  effects of 20-39

statistics 3-4, 8
  trends 1-19
tourism dependency 21
tourist sights 6-7
tourists
  behaviour 11, 31
  unconcerned about environmental impact 28-30
  visiting threatened environments 27
travel 2.0 sites 14
Travel Foundation 23
TravelTrend Watch 2008 survey 11

UK
  domestic tourism 8
  residents visits abroad 1, 4
  tourist sights 6

Virgin Galactic 12
visitors to the UK 3-4
visits abroad by UK residents 4
volunteering, gap years 15-19

wildlife trade souvenirs 32
World Vision and child sex tourism 38

Additional Resources

Other **Issues** *titles*

If you are interested in researching further some of the issues raised in *Travel and Tourism*, you may like to read the following titles in the **Issues** series:

⇨ Vol. 157 *The Problem of Globalisation* (ISBN 978 1 86168 444 8)

⇨ Vol. 151 *Climate Change* (ISBN 978 1 86168 424 0)

⇨ Vol. 150 *Migration and Population* (ISBN 978 1 86168 423 3)

⇨ Vol. 147 *The Terrorism Problem* (ISBN 978 1 86168 420 2)

⇨ Vol. 146 *Sustainability and Environment* (ISBN 978 1 86168 419 6)

⇨ Vol. 134 *Customers and Consumerism* (ISBN 978 1 86168 386 1)

⇨ Vol. 119 *Transport Trends* (ISBN 978 1 86168 352 6)

⇨ Vol. 110 *Poverty* (ISBN 978 1 86168 343 4)

⇨ Vol. 78 *Threatened Species* (ISBN 978 1 86168 267 3)

For more information about these titles, visit our website at www.independence.co.uk/publicationslist

Useful organisations

You may find the websites of the following organisations useful for further research:

⇨ **ABTA:** www.abta.com

⇨ **Different Travel:** www.different-travel.com

⇨ **ECPAT:** www.ecpat.org.uk

⇨ **Global Gateway:** www.globalgateway.org

⇨ **IIED:** www.iied.org

⇨ **i-to-i:** www.i-to-i.com

⇨ **Lonely Planet:** www.lonelyplanet.com

⇨ **The Travel Foundation:** www.thetravelfoundation.org.uk

⇨ **TravelMole:** www.travelmole.com

⇨ **VisitBritain:** www.tourismtrade.org.uk

⇨ **Voluntary Service Overseas:** www.vso.org.uk

⇨ **World Vision:** www.worldvision.org.uk

⇨ **WWF-UK:** www.wwf.org.uk

ACKNOWLEDGEMENTS

The publisher is grateful for permission to reproduce the following material.

While every care has been taken to trace and acknowledge copyright, the publisher tenders its apology for any accidental infringement or where copyright has proved untraceable. The publisher would be pleased to come to a suitable arrangement in any such case with the rightful owner.

Chapter One: Tourism Trends

Trends in the travel industry for 2008, © ABTA, Travel trends 2006, © Crown copyright is reproduced with the permission of Her Majesty's Stationery Office, Health and wellness holidays, © Mintel, Holidays are the latest status symbol, © The Press Association, Brits left cold by tourist hot spots, © Virgin Travel Insurance, Rise in specialist holidays, © TravelMole, Key UK tourism facts, © VisitBritain, New Britain, © Lonely Planet Publications, Britain's smart travellers, © TravelMole, Space tourism – the future of travel, © Telegraph Group Ltd, Space 'sports car' will take tourists into orbit, © Telegraph Group Ltd, FAQ: gap years, © TheSite, Are these the new colonialists?, © Guardian Newspapers Ltd, Ditch (un)worthy gap year causes, VSO advises, © VSO.

Chapter Two: Responsible Travel

Taking tourism to task, © Economic and Social Research Council, Thoughts on tourism, © Different Travel, Tourism and possible problems, © Global Gateway, Insider guide: sustainable tourism, © The Travel Foundation, What is ecotourism?, © i-to-i, Climate change and tourism, © Thomson Financial, Aviation's impact on the climate, © International Institute for Environment and Development, Nature's 'doom' is tourist boom, © Telegraph Group Ltd, Forget the carbon footprint, we want our summer sun, © Tiscali, Climate change could bring tourists to UK – report, © Guardian Newspaper Ltd, Lord, make us green tourists – but not just yet, © Economic and Social Research Council, British tourists among worst in world, © Expedia, Souvenir alert, © WWF-UK, Slum tours: a day trip too far?, © Guardian Newspapers Ltd, Murder, genocide and war: the new tourist attractions, © Sunday Herald, Debauchery tourism sets holiday trends, © Guardian Newspapers Ltd, Child sex tourism, © World Vision UK, Child sex tourism – FAQs, © ECPAT.

Photographs

Flickr: pages 4 (Thomas Wanhoff); 9 (Ian Muttoo); 10 (Paul L); 11 (Barry Thomas); 16 (Will Ellis); 22 (Kim Ong); 24 (Alpha); 27 (Crys); 31 (shaymus022).
Stock Xchng: pages 3 (Tim Rogers); 7 (Martin Louis); 13 (Onur Aksoy); 29 (Donald Cook); 38a (Vaughan Willis); 38b (Sophie).

Illustrations

Pages 1, 14, 25: Don Hatcher; pages 6, 23, 35: Simon Kneebone; pages 20, 33: Bev Aisbett; pages 21, 32, 37: Angelo Madrid.

Research and glossary by Claire Owen, with additional by Lisa Firth, on behalf of Independence Educational Publishers.

Additional editorial by Claire Owen, on behalf of Independence Educational Publishers.

And with thanks to the team: Mary Chapman, Sandra Dennis, Claire Owen and Jan Sunderland.

Lisa Firth
Cambridge
April, 2008